# iDentities

**PAUL SELIGSON**
LUIZ OTÁVIO BARROS with DEBORAH GOLDBLATT
and DAMIAN WILLIAMS

**STUDENT'S BOOK & WORKBOOK**
**COMBO EDITION**

**2A**

# Language Map – Student's Book

| | | Speaking / Topic | Grammar | Vocabulary / Strategies | Writing |
|---|---|---|---|---|---|
| **1** | 1.1 | What are your earliest memories of school? | | Expressions for reminiscing; Phrasal verbs with *off* | |
| | 1.2 | What innovative businesses do you know? | Subject-verb agreement: portions and indefinite pronouns; units of measurement, collective nouns, asides, and verbs as subjects | | |
| | 1.3 | How many ways can you use a brick? | | Figurative expressions for ideas (*pop into your head, hit you*, etc.) | |
| | 1.4 | What do the 2000s make you think of? | Using perfect tenses: simple past vs. present perfect; present perfect vs. present perfect continuous; past perfect vs. past perfect continuous | Uses of *set* (*put, design, establish, schedule*) | |
| | 1.5 | Have you ever had a dream come true? | | Informal responses (*That's for sure; I'll say*, etc.) | An autobiographical narrative: functions of the word *as*, both neutral and slightly more formal |
| **2** | 2.1 | What would you change about your lifestyle? | | Expressions for decision making; Expressions for expressing goals | |
| | 2.2 | What's the biggest house you've ever been to? | Avoiding repetition: affirmative and negative statements (*but I really should have; but my friends aren't*, etc.) | Plural-only nouns | |
| | 2.3 | Do you like to spend time alone? (Authentic reading: article on dining and traveling alone) | | Understanding metaphor; Common verb / adjective + noun collocations (*convey an idea, ubiquitous presence*, etc.) | |
| | 2.4 | Are you more of a morning or an evening person? | Using *so* and *such*: *so, so much, so little, so many, so few, such* and *such a(n)* | | |
| | 2.5 | Can an apartment be too small? | | Expressions from video for discussing city problems | A compare-and-contrast email: considering two things together, adding supporting points, and offering contrast |
| **Review 1** p.26 | | | | | |
| **3** | 3.1 | What language would you least like to learn? | | Expressions to discuss learning (*out of your depth, pick something up*, etc.) | |
| | 3.2 | Are you into tweeting? | Information focus: subject and object clauses (*What I did was to ... ; Why ... is unclear I'm not really sure.*) | Making your attitude clear (*to put it mildly, to say the least*, etc.) | |
| | 3.3 | Can someone learn to be a good speaker? (Authentic reading: article on public speaking) | | Expressions with *word* (*by word of mouth, get a word in edgewise*, etc.) | |
| | 3.4 | What's the ideal age to learn a language? | Using participle clauses to express result, time, and reason (*When driving to work, I used to ... ; Supported by his parents, Ben is in no hurry ...* ); Perfect participles (*Having played the trombone ...*) | | |
| | 3.5 | What can't you learn through practice? | | Expressions related to giving advice (*Practice makes perfect; You need to hit a middle ground*, etc.) | An expository essay: participle clauses for linking ideas; making suggestions with modal verbs |
| **4** | 4.1 | How often do you remember your dreams? | | Productive suffixes (*-conscious, -friendly, -related*, etc.) | |
| | 4.2 | Do you believe everything you're told? | Emphatic inversion: inverted subject and verb (*Rarely do we find such realistic sound effects, Not since ... has there been so much excitement.*) | | |
| | 4.3 | When did you last hear something illogical? (Authentic reading: article on why people believe in conspiracy theories) | | Nouns and adjectives from phrasal verbs (*break-in, throwaway*, etc.) | |
| | 4.4 | How would you describe your personality? | Formal relative clauses with *which* and *whom* (*most of whom, about which*, etc.) | | |
| | 4.5 | Would you ever hire a former criminal? | | Expressions for honesty (*be up front, on the table*, etc.) | A letter to the editor: fixed expressions to support arguments in formal writing |
| **Review 2** p.48 | | | | | |

2

# Language Map – Student's Book

| | | Speaking / Topic | Grammar | Vocabulary / Strategies | Writing |
|---|---|---|---|---|---|
| **5** | 5.1 | Why do good plans sometimes fail? | | Expressions for failed plans (*on the verge of*, *call something off*, etc.); Talking about disappointments | |
| | 5.2 | Do you ever make resolutions? | Formal conjunctions and prepositions for reason and purpose (*in view of*; *with the aim of*; *so as to*, etc.) | | |
| | 5.3 | How well do you deal with failure? (Authentic reading: article on making peace with failure) | | Expressions for evaluating success (*keep in perspective*, *take stock*, etc.) | |
| | 5.4 | Have you ever had a wrong first impression? | Levels of formality in nouns, object pronouns, and possessive adjectives + *ing* form (*I appreciated him / his considering our project*, etc.) | | |
| | 5.5 | How bad are drivers where you live? | | Expressions for making proposals (*airtight*, *rationale*, etc.) | A proposal: adverbs and adverbial expressions to link ideas and signal the next point; Formulaic expressions for formal proposals and emails |
| **6** | 6.1 | Do you still read paper books? | | Phrasal verbs with *out* | |
| | 6.2 | Do you ever watch dubbed movies? | Adverb clauses of condition (*in case*, *even if*, *as long as*, etc.) | Using the expression *out of* | |
| | 6.3 | Who are your favorite authors? (Authentic literature: short story by Roald Dahl *The Way Up to Heaven*) | | Evocative language: vivid verbs | |
| | 6.4 | What do you think of graffiti art? | Emphasis with auxiliaries (*I really did like it*, etc.) | | |
| | 6.5 | Are musicals popular where you live? | | Expressions for making recommendations | A book review: techniques and expressions to capture the reader's attention and maintain suspense |

**Review 3** *p.70*

**Grammar expansion** *p.138*  **Selected audio scripts** *p.162*

# Workbook contents

Unit 1 ............................................................................................................................................Page 3

Unit 2 ............................................................................................................................................Page 8

Unit 3 ............................................................................................................................................Page 13

Unit 4 ............................................................................................................................................Page 18

Unit 5 ............................................................................................................................................Page 23

Unit 6 ............................................................................................................................................Page 28

**Selected audio scripts** ............................................................................................................Page 63

**Answer key** ...............................................................................................................................Page 67

**Phrasal verb list** *p.119*

3

# What are your earliest memories of school?

## 1 Listening

**A** ▶ 1.1 Ben is telling his friend Lucy about a memorable experience. Look at the photos. Then listen to the first part of their conversation and guess what happened.

**B** ▶ 1.2 Listen to the second part. T (true) or F (false)? What would you have done in Ben's shoes?

1. Both the students and principal thought the lesson was fascinating.
2. Ben's lesson was interrupted by someone screaming.
3. Only some of the kids had left by the end of class.
4. Ben was hired without doing a sample lesson.
5. We know for sure that Ben was hired because of a shortage of teachers.

> I think I might have called for help. But if it had been a snake, I think I would have fainted.

**C Make it personal** Share a story about a first time.

1. ▶ 1.3 **How to say it** Complete the chart. Listen to check.

| Reminiscing | |
|---|---|
| What they said | What they meant |
| 1 As _____ as I can recall, … | From what I remember … |
| 2 I can still see it as _____ it were yesterday. | It's still fresh in my mind. |
| 3 It's completely _____ my mind. | I've completely forgotten. |
| 4 I have a vague recollection _____ … | I have a distant memory of … |
| 5 But come to _____ of it, … | In retrospect … |

2. Choose a topic from the list and note down …
   a *who, what, when, where,* and *why.*
   b which images, sounds, and smells are the most vivid.
   c any additional details.
   
   Your first …
   
   day at school    driving lesson    day in your current home    English lesson
   job interview    time speaking in public    sports event    wedding

3. In groups, share your experiences. Use *How to say it* expressions. Whose story was the most interesting?

> I'll never forget my first driving lesson. I can still see it as if it were yesterday.

> What was so unusual about it?

> I remember showing up early because I was so excited. And then just when …

♪ 'Cause the players gonna play ... And the haters gonna hate ... Baby, I'm just gonna shake ... I shake it off, I shake it off

## 2 Vocabulary: Phrasal verbs with *off*

**A** ▶ 1.4 Complete 1–6 with the correct form of these verbs. Use your intuition. Listen to check.

| doze | go | pull | rush | take | wear |

1. I even tried it for a year after I graduated from college, but the initial enthusiasm _____ off (= disappeared) after a while.
2. Yeah, I guess I don't regret that my teaching career never really _____ off (= succeeded).
3. Even the principal was yawning and looking as if he was about to _____ off (= fall asleep).
4. Anyway, it doesn't really matter because I never even had the chance to _____ it off (= make it happen).
5. Tables overturned, papers everywhere ... It was like a bomb had _____ off (= been activated).
6. Well, by then they'd all _____ off (= left in a hurry) and left me and the principal in an empty classroom.

**B** In pairs, take turns retelling the story in **1A** as if you were a) the principal, b) a student. Use at least four of the phrasal verbs.

**Common mistake**

Class is over. The bell just ~~went off~~. *rang*

**C** ▶ 1.5 Listen and complete the mind maps. Which collocations were you familiar with?

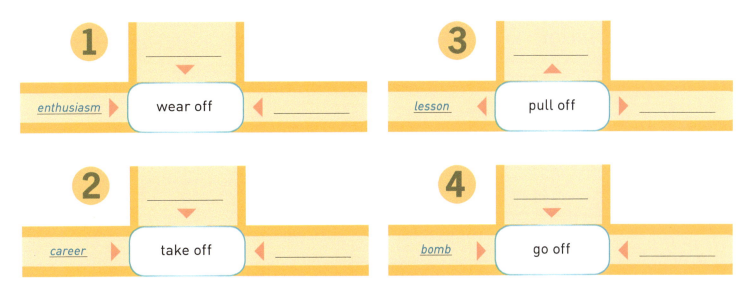

**D Make it personal** In groups, share a funny story about the last time you did something. Use phrasal verbs and collocations from **C**. Anything in common?

sat through a boring movie   were delayed traveling by bus / train / plane   managed to do something difficult
were really into a fashion or fad for a while   overslept / were late / delayed for something critical

> I had a big day coming up; a hiking date with someone I hoped would be my boyfriend. But my alarm clock never went off!

> Oh, no! Then what?

> Well, I had to think of something creative fast! So I ...

## 1.2 What innovative businesses do you know?

### 3 Language in use

**A** ▶ 1.6 Listen to the start of a podcast. What's it about?
- ☐ People who want to innovate and turn their ideas into a small business.
- ☐ Big companies that try to meet people's changing needs.

**B** ▶ 1.7 In pairs, look at the photos and the slogans. What exactly do you think each start-up does? Listen to the rest to check. How close were you?

**C** In pairs, which start-up would be more successful where you live? What kinds of problems might each one face?

> *Lists and Twists* would be a hard sell. Maybe it's just me, but I'd hate to wear something that's been worn before.

### 4 Pronunciation: Final consonant clusters

**A** ▶ 1.8 Read and listen to sentences 1 and 2. Cross out the letters you hardly hear at all, or don't hear, in the highlighted words. Then circle the correct word in the rule.

1. IT manager Elena Fernández left her job and created *Lists* and *Twists*, a company that has shipped more than 100,000 dollars in products since 2015.
2. The app asks where you're going and tracks you as you make your way to your destination – just like your parents used to do on the weekends.

A consonant cluster is a group of consonants with no vowels between them. In final clusters ending in /sts/, /kts/, /sks/, /nts/ and /ndz/, the [**first / second / third**] consonant is very weak or not pronounced.

**B** ▶ 1.9 Listen and complete 1–4 with words that end in consonant clusters. Then listen again and repeat.
1. One of our _____ _____ seven articles of clothing. ☐
2. Our team _____ new clothes based on your _____ and purchase history. ☐
3. If 60 dollars _____ like a lot of money, that's nothing compared to what most designer clothing usually _____. ☐
4. The feedback we've been getting from our _____, as well as the number of positive press reviews, _____ our commitment to excellence. ☐

**C Make it personal** Complete 1–6 to create your own innovations. Which is the class favorite?

I'd like to see a start-up / an NGO / an app / a robot that ...

inspects [1]_____ free of charge.   scans our hard disks for [2]_____ .
looks for the best discounts in [3]_____ .   lists [4]_____ in our area.
reinvents the way we [5]_____ .   defends the rights of [6]_____ .

> I'd like to see a robot that inspects my car free of charge. I'm tired of getting ripped off by mechanics!

♪ Some people want diamond rings. Some just want everything. But everything means nothing, If I ain't got you, yeah

## 5 Grammar: Subject-verb agreement

**A** Read the grammar box and complete the rules (a–c) with *singular* or *plural*.

| Subject-verb agreement: Portions and indefinite pronouns | | |
|---|---|---|
| 1 Portions and count vs. non-count | Some of the company's advertising | is very innovative. |
| | A lot of their strategies | are brilliant. |
| | A few of their apps | are unique also. |
| 2 Indefinite pronouns | No one in our group | likes my new logo. |
| | Only one of us | thinks it works. |

a *Both, many, several,* and *a few* always take a _____ verb.
b *All, any, more, most, a lot, some, a half, a third,* etc. take a singular verb when the noun is _____ and a plural verb when the noun is _____.
c *One, each, everyone, no one, someone,* and *anyone* always take a _____ verb.

**B** Read the rest. Then write the correct numbers from A and B (1–6) next to the sentences in 4B.

| Units of measurement, collective nouns, asides, and verbs as subjects | | |
|---|---|---|
| 3 Units of measurement | Sixty dollars | seems like a lot. |
| | Two months | is an eternity. |
| 4 Collective nouns | The agency | wants a deposit. |
| | In general, people | don't like having to park. |
| 5 Asides | The start-up, as well as its competitors, | is making a lot of money. |
| 6 Verbs as subjects | Having good ideas | takes a lot of courage. |

» Grammar expansion p.138

**C** Circle the correct alternative in these quotes.

1 "Everyone [**have** / **has**] talent. What is rare is the courage to follow the talent to the dark place where it leads." Erica Jong

2 "An invasion of armies can be resisted, but not an idea whose time [**have** / **has**] come." Victor Hugo

3 "One of the advantages of being disorderly [**are** / **is**] that one is constantly making exciting discoveries." Abraham Maslow

4 "Man's mind, once stretched by a new idea, never [**regain** / **regains**] its original dimensions." Oliver Wendell Holmes

5 "The achievement of excellence can only occur if the organization [**promote** / **promotes**] a culture of creative dissatisfaction." Lawrence Miller

6 "If you're having difficulty coming up with new ideas, then slow down. For me, slowing down [**have** / **has**] been a tremendous source of creativity." Natalie Goldberg

**D Make it personal** In groups, choose your two favorite quotes from C and …
1 explain what they mean and why you like them.
2 think of concrete examples to illustrate them.

> The second really struck a chord with me.

> Well, basically he's saying that …

> I'm not sure I understood it well.

## 1.3 How many ways can you use a brick?

### 6 Reading

**A** Read the first paragraph. In pairs, what creative ideas or solutions have occurred to you in the shower? List as many as you can in two minutes.

> I've figured out the solution to some crossword clues.

# The nature of creativity

You're in the shower, shampooing your hair, when – bam! – an idea pops into your head. Maybe you finally figure out a way around a problem at work. Or perhaps it becomes clear why a family member or friend has been acting out of character. Or maybe the perfect end-of-year project suddenly comes to mind. It seems that those aha! moments hit us when we least expect them and elude us when we need them the most.

Most brain research has traditionally focused on the downside of letting your mind wander, highlighting the negative effects of daydreaming on our work and academic performance. [1]But if tuning out is as bad as has been suggested, why do we spend up to 50% of our time—according to some estimates—thinking about tasks other than those in front of us? Surely this wouldn't make sense in evolutionary terms.

A few recent studies have tried to shed new light on the nature of creativity. In 2012, a team of American researchers asked 145 students to list as many uses as possible for everyday objects, for example, toothpicks and bricks. One group of participants took a break during the task and engaged in recreational, undemanding activities. When these students returned, their creative ability to think of uses for the everyday objects had improved by 41%. Creativity, it seems, requires an incubation period. [2]But are there any biological mechanisms at play here?

As it turns out, our brains are not necessarily most active when we focus and try to zero in on a task. Things that make you switch to autopilot, like showering, working out, or even scrolling through your newsfeed, tend to relax the prefrontal cortex (the "feel good" center of the brain) and release hormones that can boost creativity. In other words, when our minds wander, ideas we might never have consciously connected seem to come together. This, of course, begs the question: [3]If our brains are not wired to be constantly attentive, why is tuning out usually considered such a bad thing?

We're immersed in a culture of attention and mindfulness, which puts a premium on the ability to "stay on top of things" as we juggle busy schedules, multiple technologies, and children demanding attention. [4]How can you allow yourself to simply space out when your project is unfinished and there's a deadline looming? If recent research is anything to go by, it looks as if maybe you should. You may have the idea of a lifetime!

**B** ▶ 1.10 Read and listen. In pairs, match the questions (1–4) in the article to the most likely answers (a–e). There's one extra.

a ☐ We are expected to be focused.
b ☐ Creative ideas need time to develop.
c ☐ Students who daydream get better grades.
d ☐ It's the best way to have a creative idea.
e ☐ When you're distracted, the pleasure centers of your brain react positively.

**C** Find 1–5 in the article and circle the most likely meaning in the context.

1 elude (paragraph 1): We [**escape from** / **fail to achieve**] them.
2 shed new light on (paragraph 3): They [**explain** / **define**] it in a new way.
3 boost (paragraph 4): They [**amplify or increase it** / **push it up from below**].
4 looming (paragraph 5): It [**appears as a large form** / **is about to happen**].
5 is anything to go by (paragraph 5): It [**can be followed** / **should be obeyed**].

♪ Take you with me if I can. Been dreaming of this since a child. I'm on top of the world

1.3

**D Make it personal** In groups, debate which statements are good advice. Find evidence in the article for or against. Has anyone ever said them to you?

1 "Stop daydreaming! You won't get your homework done in time again."
2 "Take a short break. Come back to it when you're fresh, and something will occur to you."
3 "You have to learn to concentrate or you won't get ahead!"
4 "Stop worrying so much about the deadline. Let's go out and have some fun. You might have a brilliant idea!"

> My parents used to say number 1 all the time.

> But look, in paragraph 3, it says ...

## 7 Vocabulary: Figurative expressions for ideas

**A** Look at the highlighted expressions in the article in 6A. Then match them to pictures 1–6.

**B** In pairs, explain what the expressions mean. Use an online dictionary, if necessary. Then add them to the chart. Which images in A best help you remember them?

| Having an idea | Getting distracted | Staying focused |
|---|---|---|
|  |  |  |
|  |  |  |

> One meaning of *pop* is to "explode" or "burst open", so if an idea pops into your head, it "explodes" or "appears suddenly".

> Yes, like a burst of energy. So if I say, "An idea popped into my head," it means it was very sudden and wasn't there before.

**C** Share true sentences about yourself using at least three of the expressions in B.

> Yesterday when I was walking home from school, a great idea hit me ...

**D Make it personal** In pairs, share your creative process.

1 Think of a time when you couldn't think of an idea.
2 Where / When / How did the solution finally come to you?
3 Have you applied your strategy to any new situations since then? Did it work?
4 Have you ever used any of the suggestions in the article?

> I took a very demanding art course, and it was hard to stay on top of all the projects. One day, an idea just wouldn't come to me.

> So what did you do?

## 1.4 What do the 2000s make you think of?

### 8 Language in use

**A** ▶1.11 In pairs, decide the historical significance of 1–3. Then listen to a radio interview to check. Were your reasons the same?

> Wikipedia has changed the way I learn about new things.

FAMOUS FIRSTS — This week: The 2000s — BY ROY MARTINEZ

1. A non-Hollywood movie wins eight Oscars for the first time.
2. New technological words are invented.
3. The first user-created encyclopedia is introduced.

**B** ▶1.11 Read *Uses of set*. Complete 1–5 with the most logical words from the box. Listen again to check.

**Uses of *set***

*Set* is one of the most flexible verbs in English, with meanings as varied as *put*, *design*, *establish*, and *schedule*:
a  In the 90s, the Japanese **set** (= established) the standard for small cars.
b  The 2020 Olympics are **set** (= scheduled) to take place in Tokyo.
*Set* is also the verb in fixed expressions and idioms:
Nelson Mandela was **set free** (= released) in 1990.

| fire | motion | record | release | rules | stage |

1. *Slumdog Millionaire* set a new world _____: It was the first time an international production had won so many Oscars, and this set in _____ a number of important changes.
2. You may feel some of these new words didn't exactly set the world on _____ initially, but by 2010, everyone had been using words like "texting" and "to Google" for years.
3. Maybe some of these early words set the _____ for more new ones. "To Google" and "cloud computing" were invented in 2007 and "Twitter" in 2008.
4. Since it was introduced in 2001, Wikipedia has set new _____ for how we build and share knowledge.
5. I've been working on a new book, and it's different from anything I've ever written. It's set for a December _____.

**C Make it personal** In groups, do you agree with Roy's "famous firsts"? Consider these questions.
1. What percentage of films included in the Oscars should be foreign? Considering that the Academy Awards are a U.S. ceremony, how important is it for them to be international?
2. How important are language changes and the addition of new words? Was the addition of technological words a groundbreaking "first"?
3. What do you think of Wikipedia? How accurate do you think it is?

> Wikipedia definitely set the stage for a new way of accessing information.

> Yes, entries in two different languages on the same topic are sometimes completely different.

> Really? Let's try it!

♪ I'm giving you up. I've forgiven it all. You set me free

**1.4**

## 9 Grammar: Using perfect tenses

**A** Read the grammar box and check (✔) the correct rules 1–3. Find an example of each rule in 8B.

**Simple past vs. present perfect; present perfect vs. present perfect continuous; past perfect vs. past perfect continuous**

| | | |
|---|---|---|
| I | watched | the Oscars last year. |
| | 've seen | some great foreign films lately. |
| | 've been going | to the movies a lot. |
| Our view of language | has changed. | We now expect new words. |
| | has been changing | slowly. |
| I | 'd sent | a text message before I got home. |
| | had been using | the word "texting" for years when I saw it in a dictionary. |

1 When the action is complete, use the ☐ **simple past** ☐ **present perfect** if you say when the action happened.

2 The ☐ **present perfect** ☐ **present perfect continuous** sometimes means the action is complete, but the ☐ **present perfect** ☐ **present perfect continuous** always means it's in progress.

3 The ☐ **past perfect** ☐ **past perfect continuous** is used to talk about actions in progress when the action occurs before another point in the past.

» **Grammar expansion p.138**

**Common mistake**

'*ve seen*
I ~~saw~~ some great films lately. I saw a really good one at the festival.
You can only use the simple past if you say "when" or "where."

**B** Complete the discussion forum. Circle the best choice (1–7).

### WHAT ABOUT MUSIC IN THE 2010S?   Any defining moments?

**Alanis7**
To me, it was the release of Adele's *25* in 2015. Her 21 album ¹[**had been setting** / **had set**] the charts on fire a few years earlier, and no one thought she'd be able to match that kind of success. Turns out she did. *25* ²[**sold** / **has sold**] something like 3.5 million copies in the opening week alone! This is a big deal because it's shown the industry that even though album sales ³[**fell** / **have been falling**] year after year, not everybody is into singles. There's still a place for complete albums.

**TaylorFan**
Agreed. The last few years ⁴[**had been** / **have been**] pretty good for Taylor Swift, too. She ⁵[**'d won** / **won**] like a million awards in 2014–15, but, truth be told, she ⁶[**'s been breaking** / **'d been breaking**] record after record long before that.

**RiccoW**
Well, album sales are down because most people ⁷[**stopped** / **have stopped**] downloading albums. Period. Why buy an album when you can stream it on Spotify?

**C** **Make it personal** What's your most important defining moment of the 2010s?

1 🌐 Choose a topic. Search on "Top defining moments of the 2010s" for more ideas.

the arts   history   technology   sport   a personal moment

2 In groups, explain what was special about the defining moment. Use expressions with *set* as well as perfect tenses to talk about actions in the past and to bring the listener up to the present.

> For me, it was the last *Harry Potter* movie.

> What was so special about that?

> It was the end of an era. J.K. Rowling set a record for unknown writers: 40 million books translated into 67 languages and eight movies!

## 1.5 Have you ever had a dream come true?

### 10 Listening

A ▶ 1.12 Listen to Todd and Amy discussing cross-cultural relationships. Check (✔) a or b.

It can be inferred that the couple in the article …

a ☐ may not have talked about cultural differences early on.
b ☐ were aware from the beginning that culture can be very important.

B ▶ 1.13 Listen to the next part. Does Todd express these opinions? Y (yes), N (no), or NI (no information)?

1 Almost nothing is universal, and all aspects of life have to be talked about.
2 The things people say are unimportant might hide cultural assumptions.
3 People usually give up their old cultural assumptions when they move to a new country.
4 The need for security is personal, not cultural.
5 If you really try, you can change someone.

C ▶ 1.14 Guess whether the couple stayed together. Listen to the end to check. Note down two reasons for the outcome.

### 11 Keep talking

A ▶ 1.15 Read *Informal responses*. Then complete the chart. Listen to check.

**Informal responses**

In conversation, it's important to know how to respond appropriately. Some responses are neutral in register, while others can be very informal, for use with friends and family.

*I'm not sure I agree. (neutral)    You've got to be kidding! (informal)*

|  | What they said | What they meant |
|---|---|---|
| Very informal | 1 That's what I'm _____ you. | I just said that. |
|  | 2 That's for _____. OR I'll _____. | Definitely! I know. |
|  | 3 You're _____ me? How _____ I know? | I don't know. |
| Neutral | 4 Let's _____ it. | You have to consider this. |
|  | 5 Just give it a _____. | Don't decide in advance. |

B In groups, discuss these questions. Use expressions from A.

1 Did anything that Amy and Todd said surprise you? Why (not)?
2 What other sorts of conflicts can you imagine between cross-cultural couples?
3 Is a cross-cultural relationship a "first" experience you've tried or would like to try?

C **Make it personal** What unusual "firsts" have you tried? Make notes and share your story. Whose was most surprising?

**Common mistake**

*was*
It went bad / awful.

> I love danger and last summer I decided to try rock climbing. I was a little nervous, though.

> I'll bet! How did it go?

> Well, it didn't go very well.

♪ When I met you in the summer, To my heartbeat sound. We fell in love, As the leaves turned brown

1.5

## 12 Writing: An autobiographical narrative

**A** Read the narrative and answer 1–3. Underline examples.

Which tense(s) does the writer primarily use to …
1 give background information?
2 introduce and describe the events?
3 bring the reader up to the present?

**B** Read *Write it right!* Match the highlighted *as* in the narrative to the meanings 1–4 below.

### Write it right!

*As* is a versatile word that has many functions:

Slightly more formal
1 **As** we're from different cultures, Mayumi and I have some cultural differences. (= because)
2 **As** a student, I used to like French. (= when I was a student)

Neutral
3 I ran into Laura. She's working **as** a salesclerk. (= in the role of)
4 I used my jacket **as** an umbrella. (= for the purpose of)

1 because          3 for the purpose of
2 when             4 in the role of

**C** Complete these expressions with *but* from the narrative.

1 It was _____ but sheer luck.
2 I couldn't _____ but overhear.
3 I was _____ but certain.
4 I did _____ but study.

**D** Your turn! Write a four-paragraph autobiographical narrative (250 words) on a first experience.

**Before**
Plan background information, introduce and describe the events, and bring the reader up to the present.

**While**
Write four paragraphs following the model in A, adding a summary as the fourth paragraph. Be careful with narrative tenses. Include at least two examples with *as* and an expression with *but*.

**After**
Post your narrative online and read your classmates' work. Whose narrative was most surprising?

### Share your most original first experience!

### If I can do it, so can you!
By Mitch Pebble

I'd always dreamed of having a sailboat. I love the water, and as a child, I'd learned to swim by the time I was four. But I never, ever thought I'd have the chance to live on one until I moved from my home in Miami to the Caribbean island of Grenada. The most astonishing part of all is that I went there to take a temporary job as a waiter over the winter break. After that, it was nothing but sheer luck!

One night, as I was serving customers in the capital city, St. George's, I couldn't help but overhear the word "sailboat" in a conversation. Of course, my ears pricked up immediately, and I got up the courage to introduce myself. Lo and behold, it turned out that a young couple from Grenville, the island's second largest city, was looking for someone to take care of their boat as they were going to be abroad for a year. They explained that they needed an experienced "captain," who could also handle repairs. I wasn't a certified captain, and I was all but certain I had no chance at the job. Still, I couldn't let this marvelous opportunity pass, so instead of meeting friends when my shift ended, I did some research and enrolled in a sailing exam-preparation course.

I had a lot of work ahead of me, and for two months, I did nothing but study. In the end, though, I passed the test with flying colors. I had to refresh my knowledge of astronomy and meteorology. But now it's over, and I can do nautical calculations using the sun and stars as a reference. At the beginning of May, I moved … into their sailboat! My new home is a little small, and my parents are a little disappointed that I haven't gone back to school, but I've never been happier.

My friends always told me to follow my dreams, and at first, I was a little skeptical. Now I couldn't agree with them more!

### Common mistake
I had the experience of a lifetime. ~~I've~~ *I'd* never felt that way before.

Remember to maintain tense consistency in your writing.

# What would you change about your lifestyle?

## 1 Listening

**A** ▶2.1 Look at the "vision board." Guess what it is and what it's used for. Listen to the start of Luke and Julia's conversation to check. How close were you? Do you like the idea?

> It might have something to do with lifestyles.

> I wonder if it's an app.

**B** ▶2.2 Listen to the second part. Infer Luke's two main objections. Do you agree?
Luke thinks "vision boards" are ...
☐ boring.   ☐ illogical.   ☐ time-consuming.   ☐ unscientific.

**C** ▶2.3 Listen to the end. Circle the photos in A Julia talks about. Which goal(s) is she definitely going to pursue?

**D Make it personal** Talk about your own "vision board."

1 ▶2.4 **How to say it** Complete the chart. Listen to check.

| Decision-making | |
|---|---|
| What they said | What they meant |
| 1 I'm _____ (to get it published). | I'm definitely going to ... |
| 2 My _____'s made up. | I'm convinced. |
| 3 I'm _____ between (an MA in literature) and (an MBA). | I can't decide between ... |
| 4 There's a lot at _____. | There's a lot that could be lost. |
| 5 I need to give it some more _____. | I need to think about it some more. |
| 6 I've been _____ with the idea of (selling this house). | I've slowly been considering ... |

2 Think of at least four personal goals and note them down for these categories:
  a short-term (definitely)   b short-term (maybe)   c long-term (definitely)   d long-term (maybe)

3 Compare your ideas in pairs. Use *How to say it* expressions. Anything in common?

> I'm determined to take a trip abroad next year. My mind's made up! I want a freer lifestyle.

> Where will you get the money?

16

♪ You say you want a leader, But you can't seem to make up your mind. I think you better close it, And let me guide you to the purple rain

2.1

## 2 Vocabulary: Expressing goals

**A** Complete the extract from the dialogue with a–g. Check in **AS** 2.2 on p.162. Are you more like Luke or Julia?

LUKE: In other words, you're saying that a vision board really can help you ¹_____?

JULIA: Exactly.

LUKE: The whole idea seems so ²_____! You can stare at a picture of a new car till you're blue in the face, but it won't just ³_____. It's not enough just to ⁴_____. You've got to do your part and ⁵_____ – you know, save money for a long time, if necessary.

JULIA: Yes, of course, you've got to ⁶_____ your goals, even if they seem ⁷_____. But our minds help us do that.

a **go** the extra mile: make a special effort
b **work toward**: move gradually toward your objectives
c **meet** your goals: achieve your objectives
d **put** your mind to something: be determined to achieve something
e **far-fetched**: (adj) unlikely (e.g. an idea)
f **fall** into your lap: happen without any effort
g **unattainable**: (adj) cannot be reached or achieved (e.g. a goal)

**B** In groups, describe the memes in **1A** using the vocabulary from **A**. What's your (least) favorite one? Why?

> Let's see. "Goals: keep your eye on the prize." It's saying if you really work toward something, you can achieve it.

> I think that's pretty obvious.

**C** ▶ 2.5 Complete collocations 1–4 with words in red from **A**. Then listen to check. How many collocations were you familiar with?

**D** **Make it personal** Choose a collocation from **C** and a topic below. Then tell your partner something about yourself. Stop before the collocation. Can he/she guess what you had in mind?

a degree   a job problem   a personal goal   a news item   a teacher   your boss

> My boss is incredibly demanding. It's nearly impossible to meet …

> Meet her expectations?

> Exactly. Can you believe she …

17

## 2.2 What's the biggest house you've ever been to?

### 3 Language in use

A ▶ 2.6 Barry and Crystal have just moved into a new place. Listen and choose the right photo. Which one do you like better?

> I grew up in a small apartment, so I don't actually know what a big house would be like.

B ▶ 2.6 Listen again. What can you infer about Barry and Crystal? Do they remind you of anyone you know?
1 ☐ They've always lived in relatively small spaces.
2 ☐ He's probably more open to change than she is.
3 ☐ They don't work anymore.
4 ☐ Most of Crystal's friends are about her age.

C ▶ 2.7 Listen to the rest. Order Crystal's arguments about small homes 1–3. There's one extra. Do you think she convinced him?
1 ☐ more affordable
2 ☐ emotionally freeing
3 ☐ cozier
4 ☐ easier to maintain

D ▶ 2.8 Read *Plural-only nouns*. Then complete excerpts 1–4. Listen to check.

> **Plural-only nouns**
>
> Some nouns are only used in the plural. They include articles of clothing and tools / instruments that have two sides or pieces:
> jeans, pants, pajamas, shorts, glasses, earphones, scissors
>
> Other plural nouns include:
> congratulations, likes and dislikes, possessions, savings, stairs, surroundings

1 CRYSTAL: The one we kept near the _____? I threw it out.
　BARRY: You what?! I loved that painting. You did, too.

2 BARRY: I have to admit I like the _____, especially these tree-lined streets.
　CRYSTAL: I knew you would!

3 BARRY: Well, I suppose we can downsize. Especially now that we're living off our pension and _____!
　CRYSTAL: It's a new phase of life.

4 BARRY: Some of our _____ won't fit in this apartment.
　CRYSTAL: I'm sure most of them will.

E **Make it personal** In groups, answer 1–4. Any big surprises?
1 What would be your top priority when choosing a new home?
　price　size　surroundings　space for your possessions　noise　parking
2 How easy would it be for you to get used to living in a smaller space?
3 If you had one extra closet, what would you put in it?
4 Is the saying, "Less is more" always, sometimes, or never true? Why?

> Size is definitely number 1 for me. I've got tons of possessions!

> I'm not so sure. I'd put ... first.

♪ Home where my thought's escaping. Home where my music's playing. Home where my love lies waiting, silently for me

2.2

## 4 Grammar: Avoiding repetition

**A** Read the grammar box and check (✔) the correct rules (1–4). Then underline the parts of the sentences in **3D** that avoid repetition. What words are missing?

| Avoiding repetition: affirmative and negative statements | |
|---|---|
| I'm worried about finding a place to live, | but my friends **aren't**. |
| I've never lived in a house, | but my boyfriend **has**. |
| I haven't started looking for an apartment, | but I think I **might** soon. |
| I didn't rent an apartment of my own, | and I really **should have**. |
| I'd love to have more space, | but I may never be able **to**. |
| I love this neighborhood, | and my sister **does, too**. |
| I've never lived on my own, | and my girlfriend **hasn't, either**. |

1 To avoid repetition, use ☐ **a main verb** ☐ **an auxiliary or modal verb**.
2 The missing words are in the ☐ **first** ☐ **second** part of the sentence.
3 The verbs in both parts ☐ **always** ☐ **sometimes** refer to the same time period.
4 You ☐ **can** ☐ **can't** use a contracted form when the final verb is affirmative.

» Grammar expansion p.140

**B** ▶ 2.9 Cross out the unnecessary words in 1–4 and complete 5–8 with an auxiliary or modal verb. Listen to check.

**Common mistake**
*does*
I have an MBA, and my sister ~~has~~, too.

HOLLY: I didn't know you had so many CDs!
TOM: Yeah. Some are mine, and some I inherited from my brother when he went off to college.
HOLLY: Do you still listen to them?
TOM: ¹**No, I haven't** ~~listened to them~~ **in years**, ²**but I might listen to them one day**. Who knows?
HOLLY: Why would you? I mean, you're on Spotify, right?
TOM: ³**I am on Spotify**.
HOLLY: So, why don't you give them away?
TOM: ⁴**I can't bring myself to give them away**.
HOLLY: Why not? Do they bring back memories or something?
TOM: Some of them ⁵_____, yeah. This one was a gift from my grandmother.
HOLLY: *One Direction*? Do you actually like them?
TOM: I ⁶_____ when I was younger. But, you see, it's not about the music.
HOLLY: It ⁷_____?
TOM: No. It's the memory that counts! I mean, look at Grandma's note on this one.
HOLLY: Well, you could always pick the ones that mean something special and get rid of the rest.
TOM: Yeah, I guess I ⁸_____ if my brother was OK with that, too.

**C Make it personal** Your prized possessions! Role-play a conversation with a future roommate.

1 You're about to rent a very small apartment. Make a list of things you can't do without.

books    music    art / photos    clothes / shoes    appliances / devices of my own    sentimental objects

2 Decide on at least two things you will each throw out to save space. Which one was most difficult?

3 Role-play the conversation again with a new partner. Be sure to avoid repetition where possible.

I have no idea where to start.

Of course you do! What big appliances do you have?

## 2.3 Do you like to spend time alone?

### 5 Reading

**A** ▶ 2.10 Read and listen to the article. Circle the correct answer.
Its main aim is to [**describe** / **question** / **argue against**] a trend.

# Going it alone:
## more popular than ever

Travelers to the United States are sometimes struck by a phenomenon they don't see frequently at home — or, at least, one they don't think they see — the sheer number of people dining alone in restaurants. They are wrong to think this trend is limited to the U.S. In fact, it's spreading and becoming harder to miss — wherever one goes. A "single" in Amsterdam can even enjoy dining at Eenmaal, a restaurant featuring tables for one. What's more, solo dining has become common in upscale locations, as well. Long gone are the days when a diner stating "one, please" might have been ushered out of the way and into an empty room. These days, solo dining is good for business. In fact, Open Table reports that between 2013 and 2015 alone, the number of single reservations rose by 62 percent. It looks as if the solo diner is becoming more and more ubiquitous.

Another increasingly familiar presence is the solo traveler. Tour companies have gone out of their way to convey a clear message that single customers are welcome, and the success rate for their efforts is high. Among those 45 and older, according to the American Association for Retired People (AARP), more than 80 percent of those who have taken a solo trip plan to do it again.

What could possibly account for these trends? For one thing, it turns out that the number of people living alone has grown exponentially. To cite just a few examples, more than half of all homes in New York City are occupied by just one person; in London, a third; in Paris, more than half; and in Stockholm, 60 percent. As of 2012, one in five U.S. adults over the age of 25 had never been married, as opposed to one in ten in 1960. No longer a last resort, living alone has become a coveted choice for many who savor their solitude. While some singles may be avid chefs, many would rather "people gaze" than cook for just one person. As solo living has become more prevalent, solo dining has spread. And for those with a bit more disposable income, it's a short hop, skip, and jump to solo travel.

Companies planning solo tours don't only cater to those who are single, however. Increasingly, solo travelers may be half of a couple whose vacation schedules clash, or anyone who wants a taste of independence and craves new experiences. A solo vacation is, in many cases, a ticket to a week of freedom.

Where has this desire for freedom come from? Some say it may have arisen in childhood. As more children have their own rooms and spend time alone after school, they have become increasingly comfortable with a solo existence. Today, colleges are inundated with requests for single rooms. At Montclair State College in New Jersey, for example, a full 1,500 dorm rooms out of 5,000 are single rooms. Of course, it can be argued that with social media always available, students are never very far away from those they are closest to. Dining, traveling, or living on our own, it is easy enough to "reach out and touch someone," just as the phone company commercials once suggested.

**B** Sentences 1–4 are true, according to the writer. Find the evidence in the article. Do any surprise you?

1. Solo diners have become not only commonplace, but an identifiable market.
2. Children who grow up alone have less of a need for company.
3. Living alone can be a positive lifestyle choice.
4. Solo travelers are not necessarily single.

♪ What doesn't kill you makes you stronger. Stand a little taller. Doesn't mean I'm lonely when I'm alone

2.3

**C** Read *Understanding metaphor*. Then identify the metaphors in the underlined phrases in the article. In pairs, explain their meaning in that context.

> **Understanding metaphor**
>
> Authentic texts often include metaphors, where non-literal meanings are used to add power and imagery. For example: A diner might have been **ushered** into an empty room.

> Doesn't *usher*, as a verb, usually mean "to show someone to a seat," like in a theater? So here the meaning is extended to a restaurant.

**D Make it personal** In groups, what are the pros and cons of these experiences? Any disagreements?

having your own room as a child   having a roommate in college
living alone as an adult   living separately from your partner / spouse

> I can't see any advantages to couples living separately. He or she might meet someone else!

## 6 Vocabulary: Common verb / adjective + noun collocations

**A** ▶ 2.11 Complete the chart with the highlighted words in the article. Listen to check.

|   | Word | Meaning | Examples of common collocations |
|---|------|---------|--------------------------------|
| 1 | _____ | make known, communicate | an idea, a sense of (freedom), an impression |
| 2 | _____ | long for, want greatly | excitement, attention, peace and quiet |
| 3 | _____ | widespread | influence, presence, fashion |
| 4 | _____ | supply what a specific audience desires or requires | a (young) audience, (students') needs, (different) interests / tastes |
| 5 | _____ | appealing to those with money | neighborhood, restaurant, market |

**B** Complete 1–4 with collocations from **A**, changing the forms of the words as needed. Which sentences might be true for you?

> **City vs. country life: Four reasons why I went back to São Paulo!**
>
> 1 I'm not cut out for country life. When I lived in Itu, I missed São Paulo and _____ the _____ of a big city.
> 2 *Avenida Paulista*. It _____ a unique _____ of energy and freedom that's hard to put into words. Not to mention the _____ _____ of street musicians on every other corner!
> 3 How I missed the food! Not the _____ _____, but the small, affordable ones, which are just as good – and sometimes even better.
> 4 Oh, and the nightlife! It _____ everyone's tastes and _____, tourists and locals alike.

**C Make it personal** In groups, create a poster with four reasons for making one of the lifestyle changes below. Use collocations from **A**. Whose is the most convincing?

ditch social media   do yoga   never get married   save money instead of taking vacations   work from home

> I crave peace and quiet, so it would be great to work from home.

> OK, so number 1: If you crave peace and quiet, you'll never have unwanted interruptions.

21

## 2.4 Are you more of a morning or an evening person?

### 7 Language in use

**A** ▶2.12 Listen to the start of a conversation with a sleep expert. What's it about?
☐ insomnia  ☐ sleep patterns  ☐ morning routines

**B** ▶2.13 In pairs, are 1–3 good ways to start your morning? Listen to the rest to check. Were you right?
1. drinking coffee as soon as you get up
2. making your bed first thing, before taking a shower
3. checking email on your phone right after you wake up

> I see nothing wrong with drinking coffee. Do you?

**C** ▶2.13 Listen again. True (T) or false (F)? Correct the false statements.
1. It's not very important how you start your morning.
2. Postpone coffee because cortisol provides natural energy.
3. Your first task should be something achievable.
4. It's sometimes OK to skip breakfast.
5. A good time to answer email is when you first get up because you're alert.

**D** Complete what the participants said with the correct form of a word or expression from the box. Which person is most like you?

| boost (n)  drag (v)  drowsy  hectic  not sleep a wink |
|---|

  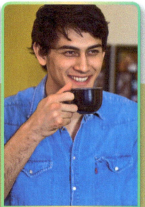  

| | | | | |
|---|---|---|---|---|
| I was such a night owl that I wrote most of my assignments between 1:00 and 4:00 a.m. Sometimes, I ¹_____ before exams! I looked like a zombie, but it was so much easier to study at night! | I looked for studies on sleep habits, but there were so few that it was hard to figure out how morning habits could ruin your day – you know, when time ²_____ and you can't think straight. | If you drink coffee as soon as you wake up, you end up with so much energy that you run out of stamina faster. But if you drink it later in the day, you get an extra energy ³_____. It's such useful advice. | You see, my mornings are so ⁴_____ I have to skip breakfast sometimes. There's just no time. In fact, there's so little I have to run for the bus. | All too often I have so little time and so many urgent messages, it's hard to put them on hold, even though I know it's not a good idea to handle email when I'm still ⁵_____. |

**E Make it personal** In pairs, what's your typical morning routine? Does it affect the rest of your day?

> In my case, I usually sleep the morning away because I'm a night owl.

> But aren't you drowsy if you have to be somewhere early?

*So many tears I've cried. So much pain inside. But baby it ain't over 'til it's over*

2.4

## 8 Grammar: Using *so* and *such*

**A** Read the grammar box and check (✔) the correct rules (1–4). Then find examples of the rules in 7D.

| *so, so much, so little, so many, so few, such* and *such a(n)* | | |
|---|---|---|
| It's | **so** comfortable | sleeping in this bed. |
| It's | **such** useful information | (that) I always remember it. |
| It makes | **such a** big difference | to wake up early. |
| It's | **so much** better | than staying up late. |
| I have | **so many** things to do | I don't know where to start. |
| There are | **so few** ways | to get a good energy boost. |
| They're charging | **so much** (money) | I can't even consider it. |
| As for free time, I have | **so little** (time) | I can barely have lunch. |

1 Use ☐ **such** ☐ **such a** before non-count nouns.
2 Use **so many / so few** with ☐ **count** ☐ **non-count** nouns, and **so much / so little** with ☐ **count** ☐ **non-count** nouns.
3 Use ☐ **so** ☐ **so much** before a comparative.
4 You can delete the noun after *so much, many*, etc.
☐ When it is in the sentence or understood
☐ only when it is in the sentence.

》 Grammar expansion p.140

**Common mistakes**

This article has such ~~a~~ useful **information / advice**.

I have such ~~a~~ strange **dreams** that I'm always scared.

**B** Complete 1–3 using the blue words in the grammar box. Then join the underlined sentences in 4–5 using the bold words and *that*.

### FIVE WAYS TO BECOME MORE PRODUCTIVE!

1 Drink more water. If you're dehydrated, you'll have _____ energy you'll barely make it through the day.

2 Use your commuting time to do something productive. There are _____ good audio books on Amazon and iTunes! You can even learn a new language while you're stuck in traffic.

3 Make yourself unavailable for a few hours, and turn off your devices, so you can work in _____ way that there are as few interruptions as possible.

4 Stop multi-tasking. Research shows <u>there are a lot of distractions invading our lives. They're changing the way our brains work</u>.

5 Have fewer and shorter meetings. <u>Long meetings waste a lot of time. Some companies have switched to stand-up meetings</u>.

**C Make it personal** In groups, share opinions on productivity.

1 What's your immediate reaction to the tips in B? Why? Use some of these expressions with words from A.

Number ___ is ¹_____ true!   Number ___ is ²_____ nonsense!
Number ___ is ³_____ a misconception!   There's ⁴_____ truth to number ___ .
Number ___ is ⁵_____ a no-brainer!

> Number 4 is such nonsense! Multi-tasking is a great way to get more done.

> Yes, but if you tried doing one task at a time, you might find …

2 When are you most / least productive during the week / day?
3 Are you as productive as you could be? If not, what would you need to change in your lifestyle?

## 2.5 Can an apartment be too small?

### 9 Listening

**A** 2.14 In pairs, brainstorm some ways your city (or one you know) has changed in recent years. Then listen to / watch (to 1:12) Shawn Groff talking about his micro apartment. Answer the questions.

1 Where does Shawn live?
2 Why has he chosen to live in a micro apartment?

> Here in ... there are a lot more people than there used to be!

**B** 2.14 Listen to / watch the second part (1:12 to 3:22). Number the reasons for micro apartments in the order mentioned. There's one extra.

a ☐ Life expectancy has increased.
b ☐ Cities are growing in size.
c ☐ More people are living alone.
d ☐ People spend less time at home than they used to.
e ☐ There is an inadequate amount of housing.
f ☐ People are marrying later and divorcing more often.

**C** 2.14 Complete 1–6 with words from the box. Listen to / watch the third part (3:22 to the end) to check.

| addressing  backlash  geared  higher  priced out  target  voiced |

1 Recent college graduates ... might otherwise be _____ of the city.
2 There has been _____ . In Seattle, community groups have _____ concerns.
3 [The apartments] are really _____ toward young, high-income people.
4 [The apartments] aren't _____ the needs of lower-middle income workers.
5 A lot of these pilots that are happening in cities are definitely on the _____ end.
6 And you can _____ different populations [with micro apartments].

**D** 2.14 Listen to / watch again (3:22 to end). In pairs, summarize two key criticisms of micro apartments. What answers to the criticisms are given? Use expressions from C.

> I think a reason there's been backlash is that ...

### 10 Keep talking

**A** Watch to 1.12 again with the sound off. Note down the features of the apartments that appeal to you most.

**B** In groups, discuss which statements in 9B are true where you live. Would micro apartments be a good solution? Which features from A might be most appealing?

> There's definitely overcrowding here, but on the other hand, I think there would be backlash if we ...

**C** Search on "innovative solutions to city problems." Share one in groups. Be sure to present the pros and cons of each solution.

> I read that in Japan, they're addressing overcrowding in Tokyo by moving jobs elsewhere.

> Yes, but what about leaving your friends and family? I think it's better to ...

♪ There are places I remember all my life, though some have changed

**2.5**

## 11 Writing: A compare-and-contrast email

**A** Read Marta's email to her friend Ann. Write the numbers of the paragraphs.

In paragraph …
a ☐ , she compares the two apartments to others available.
b ☐ , Marta first establishes that she's asking for something.
c ☐ , she mainly compares good and bad points of one apartment, but mentions a similarity for both.
d ☐ , she only compares good and bad points of one apartment.

---

**Ann Johnson** (ann.johnson@allmail.com)
**Help me decide!**

1  Hey there Ann,
Hope everything has been going well. It's been a while, hasn't it? Some big news from my end: I'm just about to rent my first apartment, and I wondered if you wouldn't mind giving me your opinion. I mean, there's so much at stake! And you always have such good practical advice!

2  I've seen two apartments. Each has its pros and cons, so my mind isn't totally made up. The first one is right in the center of town, only a ten-minute walk from my job, and the price is reasonable, too. In addition, the neighbors I've met were all very friendly. However, while the neighborhood has many amenities, including lots of stores and even a movie theater, this apartment also has some key drawbacks. For one thing, it's small and dark. Even in the morning, I'd have to keep the lights on, which would inevitably raise my electricity bill. Moreover, it's a studio apartment with tiny closets. Although there's a separate kitchen, the stove has only two burners, and there's no oven. Finally – get this (!) – one of the neighbors said he had mice last year, even though he assured me the problem has been solved!

3  The second apartment, on the other hand, is modern, light, and spacious, with a stunning view of the park. It's in an upscale neighborhood. It's also a one bedroom with fairly large closets and, of course, a full kitchen. You might say it's no contest, right? If only it were that simple. The two apartments are more or less identical in price, but the commute from the second one is horrendous. I'd have to switch trains every morning, not to mention take a bus just to get to the train. I estimate my commute would take a good hour and a half. Even so, in spite of these disadvantages, I'm thinking about it seriously. Yet it worries me that I may find I don't have much of a social life as there's very little to do in the neighborhood.

4  So what do you think? Both apartments are good deals compared to others that are available, so I'm really torn. The main difference between them would be one of lifestyle. You know me really well. You may not want the responsibility of answering this question, but where do you think I'd be happiest?

Looking forward to hearing from you. I have to leave a downpayment tomorrow!

Love,
Marta

---

**B** Read *Write it right!* Then match the underlined words or expressions in the email to 1, 2, or 3.

### Write it right!

Words and expressions used to compare and contrast fall into three categories:
1 Considering two things together: *Each has its pros and cons.*
2 Adding additional supporting points: *In addition, the neighbors I've met were all very friendly.*
3 Offering a contrast: *The second apartment, on the other hand, is modern, light, and spacious.*

**C** The modal verbs *may* and *might* can be used to speculate about the reader's reaction. Find two examples in the email.

**D** Your turn! Write a four-paragraph compare-and-contrast email (250 words) on one of the topics discussed in **10C**.

**Before**
Note down the pros and cons of both options, and decide which you will cover together in the same paragraph.

**While**
Write four paragraphs following the model in **A**, making sure to include a summary paragraph. Use expressions to compare and contrast, and at least one example of *may* or *might* to speculate.

**After**
Post your email online and read your classmates' work. Whose presents a contrast more clearly?

# Review 1
## Units 1-2

### 1 Speaking

**A** Look at the vision board on p.16.

1 In pairs, share everything you can remember about it, using these expressions.

> fall into your lap   far-fetched   go the extra mile   meet your goals   put your mind to something
> meet someone else's expectations   work toward   unattainable

2 In groups, share highlights of what you learned from your own vision boards.

> I learned I really didn't want to have to meet someone else's expectations.

3 Summarize your discussion for the class, using some of these expressions.

> a lot of us   some of us   a few of us   only one of us   no one in our group   some of us

> No one in our group has unattainable goals. ...

**B** **Make it personal** Choose three question titles from Units 1 and 2 to ask a partner. Ask at least three follow-up questions for each. What did you learn about each other?

> What are your earliest memories of school?

> I have a vague recollection of not wanting to play with anyone.

**C** 🌐 Search on "first day of school" and, in groups, make a list of the best advice.

*If you want to pull off having a totally new image, don't wear last year's clothes.*

### 2 Listening

**A** ▶R1.1 Listen to the beginning of a lecture on fashion and lifestyle. Choose the correct answer.
The main purpose of the teacher's lecture is to ...
a  describe new fashion trends in China.
b  illustrate the meaning of "lifestyle."
c  compare East and West.

**B** ▶R1.2 Listen to the whole lecture and take notes on 1–2.
1 Why is fashion important?
2 In what other areas of life might fashion trends in China lead to a more open lifestyle?

**C** **Make it personal** With a partner, share your answers to B. What does the way you dress say about your own personal lifestyle?

> Fashion is important because it ...

> I've never thought about that before, but it's true. For example, the fact that I wear ... shows that ...

Review 1
1–2

## 3 Grammar

**A** Check (✔) the correct sentences, and correct the mistake in the incorrect ones.

1 Some of this book's grammar exercises is a little difficult.
2 Two hundred dollars really are a lot for a hotel room.
3 Everyone in our class has unusual "first" experiences.
4 Only one person in my family live alone.
5 Being organized require lots of planning.
6 A few of the apps on my phone are really innovative and unusual.
7 Having new experiences, as well as learning from them, are a sign of maturity.
8 In general, most people is very impatient in stores.

**B** Make it personal In pairs, share your answers and explain the incorrect ones. Then make the sentences true for you.

> The first sentence should be "are": "Some of this book's grammar exercises are a little difficult."

> Actually, I think some of this book's grammar exercises are a little easy. But then I really love grammar!

## 4 Writing

Write a paragraph about a "first" experience a classmate told you. How much do you remember about him / her?

1 Use a range of tenses to give background information, describe the events, and bring the reader up to the present.
2 Use at least two different meanings of the word *as*.

## 5 Self-test

Correct the two mistakes in each sentence. Check your answers in Units 1 and 2. What's your score, 1–20?

1 I can picture that party yet like it were yesterday.
2 My fatigue hasn't gone off, and, in fact, I slept off in class this morning.
3 I saw some great movies lately and I've gone to a really good one last weekend.
4 Today most people stopped using their landline phones and had been using a cell phone exclusively.
5 Like we both didn't study enough, we thought the test went awful.
6 Your dream of being a chef won't seem inattainable if you really put your head to it.
7 I wasn't familiar with my new surrounding, and I fell going down the stair.
8 I didn't take the apartment, but I think I should have taken because now I'm having trouble finding a place, and my roommate has too.
9 This TV program has such a useful information and so much suggestions.
10 There are so little ways to tell the twins apart, but the main difference from them is their eyebrows.

## 6 Point of view

Choose a topic. Then support your opinion in 100–150 words, and record your answer. Ask a partner for feedback. How can you be more convincing?

a You thought the 2000s were a really innovative decade until the 2010s came along. OR
You think the 2000s definitely had more "firsts."
b You think deep down people are the same regardless of where they live. OR
You think cross-cultural relationships can be really challenging.
c You think never getting married is a valid lifestyle choice. OR
You can't imagine living and traveling alone and think marriage is a wonderful way of commiting to someone.
d You think choice of neighborhood is far more important than the size of your apartment. OR
You think a very small apartment is never worth it, even if the neighborhood is exciting.

# What language would you least like to learn?

## 1 Listening

**A** Which way of learning a foreign language (photos a–d) have you found most effective / enjoyable? Why?

> Well, I'm really into American sitcoms, but I'm not sure I've learned a lot of English from TV.

a  b  c  d

**B** ▶ 3.1 Listen to part of an English class. Which photo (a–d) best illustrates the way Hugo learned French?

**Common mistake**
*don't think*   *is*
I ~~think~~ learning grammar rules ~~isn't~~ effective.

**C** ▶ 3.2 Listen to the second part. What can you infer about Hugo, María, and the teacher? Complete 1–5 with the correct names. Check in AS 3.2 on p.162. What sentences made you decide?

1 _____ doesn't read a lot in a foreign language.
2 _____ finds language learning a challenge.
3 _____ and _____ feel hard work is essential for language learning.
4 _____ connects emotionally to English online.
5 _____ thinks living abroad makes you almost feel like a native.

**D Make it personal** In pairs, discuss 1–4. How much do you have in common?

1 Which phrase best describes your experience learning English? Why?

a bumpy ride   a necessary evil   a whole new world   Fun, fun, fun!

2 Are you more like Hugo or María? How much English have you learned through interaction? How about reading / listening for pleasure?
3 How much progress have you made in the past year in listening and speaking? Do you have any useful tips?
4 When did you first realize you could really speak English?

> Well, at first I thought English was just a necessary evil. But now it's a whole new world.

> I agree. As soon as I started understanding song lyrics, I was hooked!

♪ *Jigeumbuteo gal dekkaji gabolkka, Oppa Gangnam Style. Gangnam Style*

3.1

## 2 Pronunciation: Stress in noun / verb homographs

**A** ▶ 3.3 Read and listen to the rules and examples. Can you think of any other homographs?

> Homographs are words that have the same spelling, but may be different in meaning or pronunciation. When the pronunciation isn't the same, nouns are stressed on the first syllable and verbs on the second:
> I like to **record** (v) myself speaking English. My **record** (n) is a two-hour video!
> But many nouns and verbs are pronounced the same:
> My teacher **comments** (v) on my written work every week. Her **comments** (n) are very helpful.

**B** ▶ 3.4 Do you remember the stressed syllable in the bold words (1–5)? Listen to check. Which do you agree with?

1 I think you need to spend some time in an English-speaking country to have a really good **command** of the language.
2 I **suspect** you learn a language more easily when you're an extrovert.
3 If you're willing to go the extra mile, you can make a lot of **progress**, whether or not you're naturally good at languages.
4 Why do you need to live abroad when you can **access** the Internet and immerse yourself in a foreign language without leaving your home?
5 Reading for pleasure is the only way to **increase** your vocabulary.

> I disagree with the first one. Remember how our teacher told us she'd never lived abroad.

## 3 Vocabulary: Learning expressions

**A** ▶ 3.5 Listen to six conversation excerpts from 1B and 1C. After you hear a "beep", match each one to the teacher's response (a–g). There's one extra. Continue listening to check your answers.

a ☐ Yes, it's improved by leaps and bounds!
b ☐ You mean you picked it up naturally by talking to native speakers?
c ☐ Yes, I know you have! You've put a lot of effort into your work!
d ☐ So your French is a bit rusty …
e ☐ Well, it's natural to feel out of your depth sometimes.
f ☐ You mean you could get by?
g ☐ That's debatable.

**B Make it personal** Learning can be a bumpy ride!

1 In pairs, role-play conversations about these other learning experiences. Use learning expressions from A.

1 My serve is getting much better.
2 I really struggled when I first joined the orchestra.
3 I used to depend on my spell checker till I joined the spelling club.
4 I've worked very hard on this painting.

2 Choose at least two topics. Share true information. End by answering question 1 in 1D.

art   math   music   spelling   sports

> I've started playing the violin again. I was really rusty, but I've been putting a lot of effort into my technique.

> That's fantastic! Are you enjoying it?

> In a way I am. It's a whole new world.

29

## 3.2 Are you into tweeting?

### 4 Language in use

**A** ▶3.6 What are the blue words in the tweets called? How can they help you search for information? Listen to the start of a talk on digital literacy and check your answers.

> I think you can search by typing ..., both in Twitter and other applications like ...

1 Having lunch at Au Bon Pain. Love this place! #lunch

2 Very interesting article on global warming: www.globalwarming_whatweknow
#climatechangeisrealandweshouldactnow

3 Wonder if Rihanna thinks of Pinocchio when she sings "I love the way you lie." #funny

**B** ▶3.7 Listen to the second part. Complete a student's notes.

Reasons to use hashtags:
- Stronger messages, which reflect your [1]_____ and [2]_____ identity.
- Gives your message a humorous [3]_____
- Easier to express non-verbal [4]_____.
- Political and [5]_____ significance.
- A clearer sense of belonging to a larger [6]_____.

**C** ▶3.8 Guess the problems (a–c) for the hashtags (1–3) in A. Listen to check.

a ☐ It's hard to read.   b ☐ It doesn't offer new information.   c ☐ It assumes you agree.

**D Make it personal** What do you think of hashtags?

1 ▶3.9 **How to say it** Complete 1–6 with the words in the box. Listen to check.

extent   mildly   respects   say   speak   will

| Making your attitude clear | | |
|---|---|---|
| **What they said** | | **What they meant** |
| 1 | Hashtags let you search by topic, which, to a certain _____, filters out some of the less relevant results. | This is only partially true. |
| 2 | Hashtags are an integral part of online communication – and, in some _____, of our culture at large. | |
| 3 | What a hashtag can do is give your text more color and depth – like a clever punchline, if you _____. | I'm speaking figuratively. |
| 4 | They're just noise so to _____, and, honestly, why people use them is beyond me. | |
| 5 | This hashtag is confusing to _____ the least, and how it can help the reader isn't clear. | It's worse than I'm suggesting. |
| 6 | Personally, I find that tweet a bit lame – to put it _____ – but that's beside the point. | |

2 In groups, discuss a–d.
a Do you find hashtags helpful? How often do you use them?
b How would you improve the hashtags (1–3) in A?
c How important is it for you to get lots of likes and retweets?
d What point is the cartoon trying to make? Do you agree?

> I think the people in the building are all trying to pass the responsibility to someone else!

> I don't really agree. In the digital age ...

♪ I'm gonna raise a fuss, I'm gonna raise a holler. About a workin' all summer just to try to earn a dollar

3.2

## 5 Grammar: Information-focus clauses

**A** Read the grammar box and check (✓) the correct rules. Then underline three more examples in 4D.

### Information focus: subject and object clauses

To prepare the listener for new information, we sometimes use a subject clause:

| Subject | **How often** people post | increases their influence. |
|---|---|---|
| | **What** she did to simplify her life | was (to) unfollow lots of people. |

To explain something further, we can use an object clause:

| Object | **Why** my writing is unclear | I'm not really sure. |
|---|---|---|
| | **Whether** slang should be used | we think is a question of personal style. |

1 The verb in the information-focus clause can be ☐ **active** ☐ **passive** ☐ **active or passive**.
2 The verb starting the main clause is ☐ **singular** ☐ **plural** ☐ **singular or plural**.

» Grammar expansion p.142

**B** Correct two errors in each sentence. Can you think of any other ambiguous emoticons?

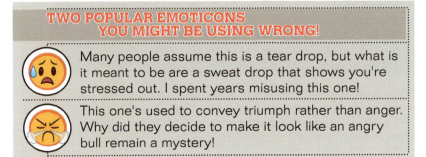

**TWO POPULAR EMOTICONS YOU MIGHT BE USING WRONG!**

Many people assume this is a tear drop, but what is it meant to be are a sweat drop that shows you're stressed out. I spent years misusing this one!

This one's used to convey triumph rather than anger. Why did they decide to make it look like an angry bull remain a mystery!

### Common mistakes

How ~~does~~ my sister ~~manage~~ *manages* to be so funny I'll never understand!

Why Bob has so many followers ~~remain~~ *remains* a mystery.

**C** Write sentences with information-focus clauses using the prompts 1–6. Use the correct tense and verb form, and add words, as needed.

**4 old-fashioned slang terms I wish would make a comeback!**

The thing about slang is that it's unpredictable. A new word or expression may catch on quickly, but ¹[how long / last / no one / know]. It may disappear in a year or two or stick around for decades. Here are four old-fashioned slang terms you might still hear:

**1** DOLL UP: I love this one! You might think it has to do with dolls, but ²[what / mean / be / "get dressed up"], as in "I got all dolled up for the party." Now, ³[how / friends / react / if / say this / mystery!]

**2** DOUGH: Slang words for "money" come and go, but "dough" is my favorite. ⁴[When / originate / surprise you]: The first printed records date back to the mid 1800s!

**3** SWANKY: If you describe something as swanky, you're saying it's expensive and fashionable. ⁵[Whether / really / be / people / decide / for themselves].

**4** WHAT'S EATING YOU? This one means "What's bothering you?" ⁶[Where exactly / hear / first time / not / remember]. It might have been in a movie. Or maybe my grandfather used it.

**D Make it personal** In groups, discuss 1–3.

1 What are the most popular slang terms right now where you live?
2 How much slang do you use? When? Where? Why?
3 Do your parents / grandparents / children ever use slang you don't recognize?

> Have you heard the expression ...?

## 3.3 Can someone learn to be a good speaker?

### 6 Reading

**A** In pairs, how do you feel when you have to speak in front of a group of people?

> I feel kind of self-conscious, but I never panic.

> Lucky you! I usually start to sweat and forget what I was about to say.

**B** Read the first paragraph. Predict at least three strategies the article might give for overcoming nervousness when speaking to a group. Continue reading to check. Were your ideas mentioned?

# Better Public Speaking:
## Becoming a Confident, Compelling Speaker
BY MINDTOOLS.COM

1   Whether we're talking in a team meeting or presenting in front of an audience, we all have to speak in public from time to time. We can do this well or we can do this badly, and the outcome strongly affects the way that people think about us. The good news is that, with thorough preparation and practice, you can overcome your nervousness and perform exceptionally well. This article explains how!

2   **Plan appropriately:** Think about how important a book's first paragraph is; if it doesn't grab you, you're likely going to put it down. The same principle goes for your speech: from the beginning, you need to intrigue your audience. For example, you could start with an interesting statistic, headline, or fact that pertains to what you're talking about and resonates with your audience. You can also use story telling as a powerful opener.

3   **Practice:** There's a good reason that we say, "Practice makes perfect!" You simply cannot be a confident, compelling speaker without practice. If you're going to be delivering a presentation or prepared speech, create it as early as possible. The earlier you put it together, the more time you'll have to practice. Practice it plenty of times alone, using the resources you'll rely on at the event, and, as you practice, tweak your words until they flow smoothly and easily.

4   **Engage with your audience:** When you speak, try to engage your audience. This makes you feel less isolated as a speaker and keeps everyone involved with your message. If appropriate, ask leading questions targeted to individuals or groups, and encourage people to participate and ask questions. Also, pay attention to how you're speaking. If you're nervous, you might talk quickly. This increases the chances that you'll trip over your words, or say something you don't mean. Force yourself to slow down by breathing deeply. Don't be afraid to gather your thoughts; pauses are an important part of conversation, and they make you sound confident, natural, and authentic.

5   **Cope with nerves:** How often have you listened to or watched a speaker who really messed up? Chances are, the answer is "not very often." Crowds are more intimidating than individuals, so think of your speech as a conversation that you're having with one person. Although your audience may be 100 people, focus on one friendly face at a time, and talk to that person as if he or she is the only one in the room.

6   **Watch recordings of your speeches:** Whenever possible, record your presentations and speeches. You can improve your speaking skills dramatically by watching yourself later, and then working on improving in areas that didn't go well. Are you looking at the audience? Did you smile? Did you speak clearly at all times? Pay attention to your gestures. Do they appear natural or forced? Make sure that people can see them, especially if you're standing behind a podium.

7   If you speak well in public, it can help you get a job or promotion, raise awareness for your team or organization, and educate others. The more you push yourself to speak in front of others, the better you'll become, and the more confidence you'll have.

© Mind Tools Ltd, 1996–2016. All rights reserved. "Mind Tools" is a registered trademark of Mind Tools Ltd.
Reproduced with permission: https://www.mindtools.com/CommSkll/PublicSpeaking.htm

♪ Drench yourself in words unspoken. Live your life with arms wide open. Today is where your book begins. The rest is still unwritten

3.3

**C** ▶ 3.10 Re-read and listen to the article. T (true) or F (false)? Underline the evidence.
1 First impressions are critical.
2 There's no such thing as too much rehearsal.
3 Audience participation can be distracting.
4 Eye contact should be random, and it's best not to look at people.
5 You can recognize and correct your own mistakes.

**D** Scan paragraphs 1–4. Find words that mean …
1 result (n): _____ (paragraph 1)
2 complete (adj): _____ (paragraph 1)
3 appeal to: _____ (paragraph 2)
4 persuasive: _____ (paragraph 3)
5 collect: _____ (paragraph 4)

**E Make it personal** In groups, discuss 1–3.
1 Who's the best / worst public speaker you see on TV? Why?
2 Which advice in the article seems most useful? Have you ever tried any of it?
3 What additional problems do people face when speaking in public in a foreign language? What can they do to cope?

> In a foreign language, you could forget words or make grammar mistakes.

> Yes, and if you have a strong accent, your audience might not understand you!

## 7 Vocabulary: Expressions with *word*

**A** Read paragraph 4 again. Underline an expression that means "to stumble" or "have trouble saying" your words.

**B** Read the quotes. Can you figure out what the highlighted expressions mean?
1 "They say 90% of the promotion of a book comes by word of mouth. But you've somehow got to get your book into the hands of those mouths first!." (Abraham Cahan)
2 "Keep your word. It creates a life of never having to explain who you are." (Cleo Wade)
3 "Happiness is a choice, not a destination. Spread the word." (Unknown quote)
4 "No, you can't take back your words. Because once you've said them, there's no refund." (Francine Chiar)
5 "I got well by talking. Death could not get a word in edgewise, grew discouraged, and traveled on." (Louise Erdrich)
6 "I believe that unarmed truth and unconditional love will have the final word in reality." (Martin Luther King, Jr.)

> I think *by word of mouth* just means "by talking." So, number 1 means you have to read the book first to be able to talk about it.

**C Make it personal** Which quotes do you agree with? How many similar opinions?

> I agree with the first. Most of the books I've read recently have been recommendations from friends.

**Common mistakes**
I couldn't get ~~the~~ *a* word in edgewise.
It spread by ~~the~~ word of mouth.
He was at a loss for ~~the~~ words.

## 3.4 What's the ideal age to learn a language?

### 8 Listening

**A** In pairs, what advantages can you imagine to growing up bilingual?

> Well, a big plus, is that you can communicate with more people.

**B** ▶ 3.11 Guess the true statements. Then listen to / watch speech pathologist Caroline Erdos to check.

1. Bilingual children solve problems more easily.
2. Later in life, bilinguals are less likely to develop Alzheimer's disease.
3. There must be only one language at home and one at school.
4. It's natural for children to mix languages, even when the parent doesn't understand both.
5. Bilingual children learn to speak a little later than monolingual children.
6. Special-needs children with language difficulties should remain monolingual.
7. To become bilingual, children need to be exposed to proficient speakers, at least 30% of the time.

Caroline Erdos

**C** ▶ 3.11 Listen / Watch again. In pairs, correct the false statements in B. Any surprises? Which facts seem the most logical?

> I was really surprised by number ... because I thought ...

### 9 Language in use

**A** ▶ 3.12 Read the discussion forum for people raised bilingual, and put 1–4 back into the posts. Listen to check. There's one extra sentence.

1. Having studied Italian informally, I've now learned the grammar
2. Taught in both languages, I felt I was always in close contact with my roots
3. Living in a city like Rio, though, I still use my German every now and then, too
4. Maybe that's why, when talking to my mom, I find it hard to discuss very abstract ideas

**B Make it personal** In pairs, answer 1–4. Any interesting stories?

1. Do you know anyone who grew up bilingual?
2. If you know bilingual people, do they mix languages? Do they switch easily from one to the other?
3. Do you think bilinguals have a favorite language? Do they think mainly in one?
4. Do you agree with the video that bilingualism has only advantages?

> I'm not sure I agree with number 4. I knew this guy who couldn't speak either language well.

> But did he have enough input? Remember the video said that ...

**Anita**: Having been raised in Brazil by an Australian mother and German father, I learned how to navigate between languages comfortably from a very early age. Today, I use both Portuguese and English at work. _____, even if it's only to help tourists with directions and things like that.

**Fred**: I grew up in Chicago, speaking English with my dad and Italian with my mom, almost exclusively. When I went to school, my English surpassed my Italian, of course. _____ My conversations with Dad, on the other hand, tend to be more profound – unless, of course, I switch to English with Mom.

**Marco**: Growing up in a multicultural home in Buenos Aires, I've always cherished my heritage. My mother is Argentinean, and my dad is American. We spoke both English and Spanish at home, and when I was six, my parents enrolled me in a bilingual school. Looking back, it was the best thing they could have done. _____

♪ And promise you kid that I'll give so much more than I get. I just haven't met you yet

3.4

## 10 Grammar: Using participle clauses

**A** Read the grammar box and check (✔) the correct rules (a–c).

> **Participle clauses to express result, time, and reason**
> 1 **Knowing** some English, | I never have trouble getting by.
> 2 **Growing up** in a family of artists, | Gwen eventually became an actress.
> 3 **When driving** to work, | I used to listen to audio books.
> 4 **Supported** by his parents, | Ben is in no hurry to find a job.
>
> Participle clauses, which are very common in written English …
> a describe the ☐ **past** ☐ **present or past**.
> b refer to the ☐ **subject** ☐ **object** of the main sentence.
> c are ☐ **always active** ☐ **either active or passive**.

»  Grammar expansion p.142

**B** Choose the correct meaning (a–d) for the example sentences (1–4) in the grammar box. Then rephrase the participle clauses 1–3 in **9A** beginning with a conjunction, too.

a As I [**know** / **knew**] some English, I …
b She [**grew up** / **is growing up**] in a family of artists, so …
c When I [**drive** / **drove**] to work, I …
d Because he [**is** / **was**] supported by his parents, he …

> **Common mistake**
>
> *I spent a lot of time writing*
> Growing up as only child, ~~my time was spent writing~~.
>
> Participle clauses must have a clear subject: Your time didn't grow up – you did.

**C** Complete 1–5 with participle clauses, using the verbs in the box.

| begin | educate | inspire | watch | win |

**The apple doesn't fall far from the tree**

① _____ her mother perform across the globe for decades, singer and actress **Liza Minnelli** went on to become one of the world's most successful entertainers.

② _____ by his grandfather's collection of jazz records, crooner **Michael Bublé** decided he wanted to become a singer at a very early age.

③ _____ his musical career at the age of five with a story on Yoko Ono's 1981 album, *Season of Glass*, **Sean Lennon** went on to become a musician and singer in his own right.

④ **Laila Ali**, daughter of world champion Muhammad Ali, became a professional boxer at age 18. _____ all the fights she ever took part in, **Laila Ali** retired from the ring in 2007.

⑤ _____ in Miami from the age of seven, **Enrique Iglesias**, son of Spanish singer Julio Iglesias, sings in both Spanish and English.

**D** Read *Perfect participles*. Then rephrase 1–5 in **C**.

> **Perfect participles**
>
> You may use a perfect participle to emphasize that an action happened before another one:
> **Having played** the trombone when I was younger, I already knew how to read music.
> **After having graduated**, I started looking for a job in my field.

**E** **Make it personal** In groups, answer 1–3. Any interesting stories?
1 List a few of your special skills, talents, and accomplishments.
2 Which did you pick up mostly from your (a) family, (b) friends, (c) teachers?
3 Do you know anyone with a special talent that became clear early in life?

> Yes, my nephew started writing music when he was just 12. Growing up in a musical family, he was exposed to music all the time.

35

## 3.5 What can't you learn through practice?

### 11 Listening

**A** ▶ 3.13 Listen to part one of a conversation between two friends, David and Paula. In pairs, answer 1–2.
1 What did the musician do during the concert?
2 Why did he do it?

**B** ▶ 3.14 Listen to part two. Then check (✔) Paula's advice, a or b. Do you agree with her reasons?

1 a ☐ Think about your audience during a performance. You need to be concerned with people's reactions.
  b ☐ Don't worry too much about your audience. People tend to be more accepting than we give them credit for.
2 a ☐ Don't try too hard. It will just make you nervous.
  b ☐ Try to do the best you can. It's important to be good, but within reasonable limits.
3 a ☐ Don't focus on talent. Learning is mainly motivation and practice.
  b ☐ Consider if you have talent. If not, choose something else to learn.

**C** ▶ 3.15 Fill in the missing words in these expressions. Listen to check.
1 Practice makes _____, remember?
2 I really have my _____ about my playing! I can't even _____ to imagine giving a concert.
3 You're setting yourself impossibly high _____.
4 Don't go to the other _____. You need to hit a middle _____.
5 Do your very _____, but don't worry about being perfect.
6 Do you think I could learn to ski if I put my _____ to it?
7 Yeah, I do. Why not give it a _____?

### 12 Keep talking

**A** Choose or invent something you've been <u>unable</u> to learn. Think about these questions:
1 Why did you have trouble learning it?
2 How often / hard did you try?
3 Might you give it another shot in the future?
4 What would you do differently?

**B** In groups, take turns presenting your problem for the others to offer advice. Use the expressions in **11C** and those below.

> In addition to ..., you might want to ...   Have you thought about ...?
> You might not ..., but you can still ...

> I've been unable to learn how to swim! I can't even begin to imagine being in the deep end of the pool. Maybe you can give me some advice.

> Have you thought about relaxation techniques? Maybe you're scared.

"I CAN'T READ BUT I HAVE EXCELLENT TV VIEWING SKILLS."

36

♪ There's nothing you can do that can't be done ... It's easy. All you need is love

3.5

## 13 Writing: An expository essay

**A** Read the essay on an online site for language learners. Find ...

1 a sentence that creates initial interest.
2 the topic sentence.
3 three concrete techniques the essay offers.

**B** A good expository essay maintains the theme in a paragraph. In paragraphs 3–5 underline seven time words and expressions that help link ideas.

**C** Read *Write it right!* Then find three more participle clauses that the writer uses to link ideas. What is the subject of each one?

> **Write it right!**
>
> Expository essays use a variety of structures to create interest. Participle clauses with *-ing* are one way to link ideas or create suspense.
> **Before downloading** a full album, I would look at the lyrics to see if the language seemed "useful."

**D** Combine 1–5 with participle clauses. Check all sentences to be sure the subject is clear!

1 You need to be motivated. In addition, you need to go the extra mile.
   *In addition to being motivated, you need to go the extra mile.*
2 I love listening to music. My friends tell me I can improve my English that way.
3 I bought some new albums. I started to listen to them every day.
4 I imagined visual scenes as I listened. I felt as if I was in the U.S.
5 I've learned a lot more colloquial language. My listening skills have improved.

**E Your turn!** Choose a topic you role-played in **12** and write an essay giving three pieces of advice in about 280 words.

**Before**
Choose three pieces of advice. Note down details to support your arguments.

**While**
Write six paragraphs following the model in **A**. Use at least two participle clauses and two other linking words or expressions.

**After**
Post your essay online and read your classmates' work. Who had the best advice?

---

### What worked for me when I was studying Russian

1 We've all seen announcements from language programs that promise we can learn English (or another language) in "twenty easy lessons." Naturally, that's false. But you might well be wondering what exactly the best way to learn a language really is.

2 Just as there are multiple kinds of intelligences, there are multiple ways of learning a foreign language. Your personal techniques have a lot to do with your personality and your learning style. What you need is lots of patience – and, of course, motivation. These three techniques helped me tremendously with Russian, my college major.

3 I'm the kind of person who likes to listen. In fact, my friends tell me I'm a good listener, and they often choose me when confiding their problems. So, I decided to apply my listening skills to learning Russian. First, I had some Russian friends recommend popular music to me. Before downloading a full album, I would look at the lyrics to see if the language seemed "useful." Then listening to the songs over and over, I would compare the lyrics with the English translation I had also downloaded. Over time, I started to pick up new words and expressions, and what's more, I even heard them used when I had a chance to practice my Russian with native speakers.

4 As well as focusing on music, I thought TV could be useful for language learning. So even though I don't really like TV, I decided to pay extra to have access to the local Russian channel, too. Then I began to watch movies with the English subtitles on. In the beginning, I understood very little. The actors talked so fast! But in no time at all, I started to follow the dialogue because my favorite soap opera had a predictable plot.

5 There was no way I was going to do grammar exercises in my free time, but I love to read. So, after a while, in addition to listening to music and watching TV, I decided to read novels to improve my grammar. I would look closely to see if I could recognize the structures taught in class, and sometimes made a mental note to use parts of sentences myself in conversation. In a matter of weeks, I was trying out new expressions! You could try this technique, too. But be careful! It only works with modern novels. If you read Tolstoy or Dostoyevsky, you may start sounding as if you were born in the 1820s!

6 These are just a few fun and useful ways you can improve your language skills in any language. You might want to try them, too!

# How often do you remember your dreams?

## 1 Listening

**A** ▶4.1 Listen to the start of a radio show with a psychologist. Circle the correct answer.

Scientists [**are fairly sure** / **only suspect**] that some dreams may reveal certain things about our personalities.

**B** ▶4.2 Guess what dreams 1–3 represent. Listen to the second part and write the numbers. There's one extra choice. Any surprises?

- ☐ anger
- ☐ perfectionism in your work
- ☐ anxiety or guilt
- ☐ unassertiveness

1     2     3

**C** ▶4.2 Listen again and complete the chart.

| In which conversation(s) does Dr. Wallace … | 1 | 2 | 3 |
|---|---|---|---|
| 1  reassure the caller things will be OK? | | | |
| 2  offer two different interpretations of the same dream? | | | |
| 3  ask for further details about the dream? | | | |
| 4  avoid committing to a point of view? | | | |
| 5  seem to have trouble convincing the caller? | | | |

**D** ▶4.3 Listen to the end of the show. Summarize Dr. Wallace's last point in one sentence.

**E Make it personal** In pairs, discuss these questions.

1  Have you ever had a dream that came true? What happened?
2  Have you recently dreamed about …?

fire   water   flying   falling   being trapped
being unable to move   missing a plane/train   failing in school

> **Common mistake**
> *about*
> I dreamed ~~with~~ falling last night.

3  🌐 Search online for an interpretation. Does it make sense?

> I've had dreams about falling, but I don't feel insecure and anxious like the website says.

> It can mean other things, too. Maybe you were afraid of failing at love.

38

♪ Never forget where you've come here from. Never pretend that it's all real. Someday soon this will all be someone else's dream

4.1

## 2 Vocabulary: Productive suffixes

**A** ▶4.4 Read about productive suffixes. Then complete 1–6 with the correct suffixes. Listen to check. Where does the stress fall?

Unlike suffixes such as *-ment, -ous, -al*, which usually change word class (for example, *enjoy, enjoyment*), productive suffixes can be used to create brand new words:

| Suffix | Definition | Example |
|---|---|---|
| ___-friendly | helpful or safe | a user-friendly interface |
| ___-conscious | concerned about | a politically-conscious artist |
| ___-oriented | directed at, focused on | a consumer-oriented company |
| ___(-)like | similar to | a lifelike portrait |
| ___-related | connected with | an age-related disease |
| ___worthy | deserving of something | a newsworthy event |

1  The book is thoroughly researched and very reader-_____ at the same time.
2  Your review of the current literature on dreams is especially praise _____.
3  Highly competitive, results-_____ individuals often have this sort of dream.
4  It really sounds as if your nightmare is stress-_____.
5  I have a recurring dream of being chased through the woods by a tall, ghost-_____ figure.
6  The more image-_____ we are, the worse it gets.

**B** In pairs, take turns thinking of an example for each item in column 3. Share opinions.

> I think the iPhone has a very user-friendly interface.

**C** Reword the phrases in italics with a suffix from **A**.
1  *People who are concerned about their health* aren't fun to hang out with.
2  *A leader that you can trust* is almost impossible to find these days.
3  *Teaching that is directed at exams* does students more harm than good.
4  *Entertainment that's safe for the whole family* is almost impossible to find these days.
5  *Programs connected with school* are a great way for kids to develop independence.

> I'm not sure. I think Androids are slightly more user-friendly.

**D Make it personal** Are you set in your ways? What fixed opinions do you have?

1  ▶4.5 **How to say it** Complete the chart. Listen to check.

| Committing to a point of view |||
|---|---|
| **What they said** | **What they meant** |
| 1  I wouldn't go so _____ as to (call it a masterpiece). | I wouldn't go to the extent of … |
| 2  The _____ is still out on (whether that's true). | There's no agreement that … |
| 3  There's no _____ in my mind that (they will). | I'm absolutely sure that … |
| 4  Oh, yes, without a _____ of a doubt. | I'm positive. |
| 5  We should take (these claims) with a grain of _____. | We should be skeptical of … |

2  Choose two statements from **2C** you feel strongly about. Note down a few ideas under "I'm convinced that …"/ "I'm not entirely convinced that …"
3  In groups, share your ideas. Use *How to say it* expressions. Any major disagreements?

> OK, number 1: "Health-conscious people aren't fun to hang out with" … Hmm, I wouldn't go so far as to call them boring, though.

> Well, not unless they try to change your eating habits.

39

## 4.2 Do you believe everything you're told?

### 3 Language in use

**A** ▶ 4.6 Use the photos and speech bubbles to guess what happened. Listen to check. Then choose the correct option in the heading.

The greatest [prank / misunderstanding] of all time!

*Little did he know it would scare millions of people.*

*Not only did the creatures look hideous, they were evil, too.*

*Never before had a radio show caused so much panic.*

*Only when he realized the seriousness of the situation, did he interrupt the show.*

Didn't *The War of the Worlds* begin as a radio show?

Yes, with actor Orson Welles. I think it might have been about ...

**B** ▶ 4.6 Number the events in order (1–5). Listen again to check. Then look in AS 4.6 on p.162. Underline phrases that helped you decide.

- [ ] People tried to escape from their homes.
- [ ] Listeners discovered the truth and relaxed.
- [ ] The radio station learned about the impact of the show.
- [ ] The show was heavily criticized.
- [ ] News of the killer aliens scared listeners.

**C** ▶ 4.7 Match each verb (1–5) with an object (a–e). What does each phrase mean? Listen to check. Which two verbs are used figuratively?

1 throw         a ☐ a sigh of relief
2 clog          b ☐ havoc
3 flee          c ☐ someone into a frenzy
4 breathe       d ☐ the attack
5 wreak         e ☐ the highways

**D** In pairs, take turns telling the story from memory. Use expressions from **C**, making sure you know the past forms, too.

**E** **Make it personal** Have you, or has anyone you know, ever believed a science-fiction story about one of these topics? What happened as the result?

mythical creatures    the end of the world
natural disasters     transportation

*When I was a kid, I believed a dragon could fly in our window. I really thought I might have to flee an attack!*

♪ Never in my wildest dreams, Did I think someone could care about me

4.2

## 4 Grammar: Emphatic inversion

**A** Read the grammar box and check (✔) the correct rules.

| Emphatic inversion: Inverted subject and verb | |
|---|---|
| *Rarely* **do we find** | such realistic sound effects. |
| *Little* **did they know** | what the show would cause. |
| *Nowhere* **could they find** | the cause of the panic. |
| *Only after* the scandal had blown over, | **was he** asked to direct *Citizen Kane*. |
| *Not since* CBS aired the show, | **has there been** so much excitement. |

1 Inversion is used with adverbs and adverbial expressions to ☐ emphasize ☐ de-emphasize what you are saying. It is especially common in writing.
2 Whether inversion is possible is determined by the ☐ topic ☐ adverb or adverbial expression.
3 With *only after / when, not since*, etc., inversion is always in the ☐ first ☐ second clause.
4 The adverbials in italics have a ☐ positive ☐ negative or, in some cases, limiting meaning.

**Common mistakes**

Only when ~~did I watch~~ *I watched* the movie, did I appreciate it.
Not only ~~I watched~~ *did I watch* it six times, but I memorized the script.

» Grammar expansion p.144

**B** Circle the correct answers in column B. Then rephrase the sentences from 3A so they are neutral.

### Orson Welles' *Citizen Kane*: What the reviewers have said

| A: Neutral | B: Emphatic |
|---|---|
| 1 There'll never be such an excellent script again! | Never again [**will there be** / there will be] such an excellent script. |
| 2 You'll only fully appreciate this movie when you watch it. | Only when [**you watch** / do you watch] this movie, [you will / **will you**] fully appreciate it. |
| 3 Critics have rarely voted a film "the greatest film of all time." | Rarely [**have critics voted** / critics have voted] a film "the greatest film of all time." |
| 4 There hasn't been such a critical success since the movie came out. | Not since the movie [did come out / **came out**] [**has there been** / there has been] such a critical success. |

**C** Rewrite 1–4 starting with the adverbials in parentheses. What was your favorite prank?

### The most epic April Fools' day pranks of all time!

**2015:** A train company announced that it had plans to replace conventional seats with state-of-the-art gym equipment. (1) *Train travel would no longer be sedentary* (no longer)!
**1992:** Passengers approaching Los Angeles airport were shocked to see a huge banner welcoming them to Chicago! (2) *They only realized it was a prank after the plane had landed.* (only after)
**1980:** A TV station reported that London's iconic Big Ben was going to be turned into a digital clock.
   (3) *People were not only shocked, but they were also outraged.* (not only)
**1957:** A news program had convinced viewers that spaghetti could grow on trees.
   (4) *There had not been such a creative prank since the invention of TV.* (not since)

**D** 🌐 **Make it personal** Search on "April Fools' pranks" and share your best two in groups. Which one was funniest?

This guy bought colored post-it notes and covered his friend's car. So not only did she not recognize her own car, but she also thought it was a wedding decoration.

41

## 4.3 When did you last hear something illogical?

### 5 Vocabulary: Nouns and adjectives from phrasal verbs

**A** Read *Synonyms for nouns and adjectives from phrasal verbs*. Then circle five more examples in the headlines below and draw an arrow connecting them to their synonyms.

> **Synonyms for nouns and adjectives from phrasal verbs**
>
> Nouns and adjectives formed from phrasal verbs often have neutral or slightly more formal one-word synonyms:
> We've had two burglaries this year. I'm of tired of these break-ins (n). We need to beef up security. (= Someone **broke in**.)
> Even computers can be disposable. Most companies these days are producing throwaway laptops with cheap plastic bodies. (= That we **throw away**.)
>
> Remember: Some words formed from phrasal verbs are hyphenated, and some are one word. The stress is on the first syllable.

### Our favorite "conspiracy headlines" of the past few years

Conspiracy theories are more pervasive than ever before on social media.

| KIND OF CONSPIRACY | TYPICAL HEADLINE |
| --- | --- |
| 1 Earth's imminent destruction | Total wipeout of the planet likely due to solar storm in 2023. So far, no precautions taken! |
| 2 Restriction of our personal freedom | Sales of surveillance cameras up by 80%: Crackdown on civil liberties "worse than ever before," study suggests. |
| 3 Concealment of official information | The cover-up of the decade: Cure for cancer available at least since 2002. |
| 4 Control by evil creatures accelerates | Illuminati takeover enters its final phase. |
| 5 Confidential warning about dead celebrity sightings | "English singer David Bowie is alive and well," tip-off reveals. |

**B** Complete 1–5 with the phrasal verb form of the words you circled in the headlines in **A**. Then change the sentences, if necessary, so they're true for you.

1 Where I live, if you witness a crime, it's easy to _____ _____ the police anonymously.
2 The police should _____ _____ on graffiti artists. Enough is enough!
3 I suspect the truth behind the side effects of many drugs has been _____ _____ by drug companies.
4 I'm not entirely convinced dinosaurs were _____ _____ by an asteroid.
5 I'm sure tech companies are trying to _____ _____ the world.

> I doubt tech companies are trying to take over the world. They're only offering products we want.

**C Make it personal** In pairs, answer 1–3. Who's more skeptical of conspiracy theories?

1 Which conspiracy theories from 3 are you familiar with? Which are the most outlandish / plausible?
2 🌐 Search online for conspiracy theories. Share your favorite ones.
3 Why are some people attracted to these theories?

> I think some people are suspicious by nature, and so they love these kinds of theories.

♪ But then they sent me away to teach me how to be sensible. Logical, responsible, practical

**4.3**

## 6 Reading

**A** Read paragraph 1 of the article. How would the author answer question 3 in **5C**?

☐ Because they have a natural tendency to look for meaning in random events.
☐ Because the evidence the theories are based on can be misleading.

---

### Why Do Some People Believe in Conspiracy Theories?

Christopher French, a professor of psychology at Goldsmiths, University of London, explains:

Although conspiracy beliefs can occasionally be based on a rational analysis of the evidence, most of the time they are not. As a species, one of our greatest strengths is our ability to find meaningful patterns in the world around us and to make causal inferences. We sometimes, however, see patterns and causal connections that are not there, especially when we feel that events are beyond our control.

The attractiveness of conspiracy theories may arise from a number of cognitive biases that characterize the way we process information. "Confirmation bias" is the most pervasive cognitive bias and a powerful driver of belief in conspiracies. We all have a natural inclination to give more weight to evidence that supports what we already believe and ignore evidence that contradicts our beliefs. The real-world events that often become the subject of conspiracy theories tend to be intrinsically complex and unclear. Early reports may contain errors, contradictions and ambiguities, and those wishing to find evidence of a cover-up will focus on such inconsistencies to bolster their claims.

"Proportionality bias," our innate tendency to assume that big events have big causes, may also explain our tendency to accept conspiracies. This is one reason many people were uncomfortable with the idea that President John F. Kennedy was the victim of a deranged lone gunman and found it easier to accept the theory that he was the victim of a large-scale conspiracy.

Another relevant cognitive bias is "projection." People who endorse conspiracy theories may be more likely to engage in conspiratorial behaviors themselves, such as spreading rumors or tending to be suspicious of others' motives. If you would engage in such behavior, it may seem natural that other people would as well, making conspiracies appear more plausible and widespread. Furthermore, people who are strongly inclined toward conspiratorial thinking will be more likely to endorse mutually contradictory theories. For example, if you believe that Osama bin Laden was killed many years before the American government officially announced his death, you are also more likely to believe that he is still alive.

None of the above should indicate that all conspiracy theories are false. Some may indeed turn out to be true. The point is that some individuals may have a tendency to find such theories attractive. The crux of the matter is that conspiracists are not really sure what the true explanation of an event is – they are simply certain that the "official story" is a cover-up.

---

**B** ▶ 4.8 A *cognitive bias* is a tendency to confuse our subjective perceptions with reality. Listen to and read the article. Match the quotes (1–3) to the types of cognitive bias in the article (a–c).

| a confirmation bias   b proportionality bias   c projection |

1 ☐ "I'm sure our politicians are spying on us. If I were in charge, I'm sure I would do the same."
2 ☐ "A legend like David Bowie couldn't have died just like that without our knowing he was sick. Something smells fishy."
3 ☐ "I get severe headaches whenever I use my phone a lot. I've always believed in the the dangers of radiation."

**C** Read *Tentative language*. Underline two examples in each paragraph in the article.

> **Tentative language**
>
> Academic writing is **often** based on hypotheses and interpretation. Therefore, **most** writers **tend** to avoid making generalizations and being too assertive, which **might** put readers off. The words in bold (e.g. modals, adverbs, quantifiers) are examples of how writers use tentative language to show they aren't 100% certain.

**D Make it personal** What are *your* biases?

1 In groups, read each word in turn and say <u>the very first word</u> that comes to mind.

> cooking   fitness   Hollywood   smartphones
> Lady Gaga   politics   soccer   taxi drivers

2 Which words, if any, reveal(s) a hidden bias?

> Taxi drivers conjure up images of speeding!

> I think that's biased. Some drive very carefully.

## 4.4 How would you describe your personality?

### 7 Language in use

**A** Look at the eyes and pick the one you're immediately drawn to. Then search on "eye personality test" and read the results on one of the sites you find. Are they accurate for you?

> I chose the first one. It says I'm an open, kind spirit who welcomes everyone into my life.

**B** ▶ 4.9 Listen to the start of an interview with a psychologist. How does he feel about the test in A? Do you agree?

**C** ▶ 4.10 Listen to the rest. Why is he skeptical of personality tests? Check (✔) the points he makes.

1 People's personalities …
a ☐ are sometimes contradictory.
b ☐ are influenced by life events.
c ☐ can be captured better in interviews than tests.

2 Employee personality tests …
a ☐ haven't been updated in years.
b ☐ may be used inappropriately.
c ☐ can't predict performance accurately.

**D** ▶ 4.11 Read *Pronouncing the letter s*. Then write /s/ or /z/ next to the highlighted letters in 1–4. Listen to check.

> **Pronouncing the letter s**
>
> The letter *s* is tricky. We say *assume* /s/, but *possess* /z/; *base* /s/, but *phase* /z/. These simple rules will help you. Say …
> - /s/ in the suffix *sis*: *basis* and in the prefix *dis*: *disadvantage*.
> - /z/ in the suffix *sm*: *sarcasm*.
> - /z/ for a verb (*use* a pen) and /s/ for a noun or adjective (make *use* of it) in homographs.

1 It depends on the kind of research on which the test was ba**s**ed ☐ and on the subsequent data analy**s**is ☐.
2 The web is full of amateur tests, all of which have come in for a lot of critici**s**m ☐ in recent years.
3 These tests provide vague personality descriptions, with which it's hard to di**s**agree ☐.
4 I interviewed over a hundred recruiting managers, some of whom admitted to using test results as an excu**s**e ☐ not to hire or promote someone.

**E Make it personal** In pairs, how do you feel about …? Be sure to pronounce the bold words correctly.

fad diets   faith-healing   fortune-telling   horoscopes   self-help books   telepathy

> I (don't) think … make(s) sense. I can('t) understand people's **skepticism**!
> Once I … and I was(n't) **disappointed**. What happened was …
> Most of my friends would **disagree** with me, but …
> The **hypothesis** that … sounds … to me. For one thing …
> I don't think you can **use** … to …

> Most of my friends would disagree with me, but I don't think you can use the argument that fad diets are better than no diet.

♪ I don't wanna close my eyes, I don't want to fall asleep. 'Cause I'd miss you baby and I don't want to miss a thing

4.4

## 8 Grammar: Formal relative clauses

**A** Read the grammar box and complete rules 1–3. Then look at 1–4 in 7D and say which nouns *which* and *whom* refer to.

### Formal relative clauses with *which* and *whom*

| A hundred **people** were surveyed, | **most of whom** regularly take personality tests. |
| Most tests are based on **theories** | **about which** very little is known. |
| I'd like to thank **Dr. Cooper**, | **without whom** this study wouldn't have been possible. |
| I prefer to read **books** and **articles** | **from which** I can derive new insights. |

In formal relative clauses ...
1. the preposition goes _____ the relative pronoun.
2. we use the pronoun _____ for people and _____ for things.
3. a non-restrictive clause is preceded by a _____ .

» Grammar expansion p.144

**B** Unscramble the bold words in 1–6 using formal relative clauses. There's one extra word in each group.

**Common mistake**
✓ (that) the movie is based **on**. (neutral)
✓ **on which** the movie is based. (more formal)
This is the book (that) the movie is based.

### The "Big 5"

The Five Factor Model is based on the idea that there are five broad domains ¹[which / our / can / personalities / that / into / be / classified]:

**1 Openness to experience:** This describes the extent ²[which / to / what / someone / curious / is], imaginative, and adventurous. Can he or she "think outside the box?"

**2 Conscientiousness:** Reliability, thoroughness, and self-discipline are traits ³[whom / with / often / is / conscientiousness / which / associated].

**3 Extroversion:** Extroverts thrive on social interaction and seek the company of people ⁴[who / exchange / can / they / with / ideas / whom].

**4 Agreeableness:** These individuals, ⁵[on / which / we / count / usually / whom / can] in times of trouble, tend to be kind, cooperative, and sympathetic.

**5 Neuroticism:** This trait refers to the frequency ⁶[that / with / an / which / experiences / individual] negative emotions. e.g anxiety, anger, or depression.

**C** Complete the survey results with *which*, *whom*, and a preposition. How would *you* personally rank 1–5?

| What do you value the most when choosing a boyfriend / girlfriend? Our survey results: | Number 1 for % of responses |
|---|---|
| 1 The kindness _____ _____ they treat pets. | 15 |
| 2 The creativity _____ _____ they approach their job. | 25 |
| 3 The friends _____ _____ they surround themselves. | 55 |
| 4 The sense of ethics _____ _____ they base their lives. | 75 |
| 5 The people _____ _____ they show empathy. | 90 |

**D Make it personal** In groups, answer the question and list at least three qualities or characteristics. Use formal relative clauses where possible. Similar opinions?

What do you value the most when choosing a(n) ...?

> Doctors? I value the empathy with which they treat their patients.

airline    bank    doctor / dentist    friend    language school    roommate    vacation spot

## 4.5 Would you ever hire a former criminal?

### 9 Listening

**A** ▶4.12 In pairs, guess two reasons for 1–2. Then listen to the first part of a conversation between Julie and Seth to check.

> Should an employer have a right to know if an applicant has a criminal record?
> 1 Yes, because …   2 No, because …

**B** ▶4.13 Listen to the rest. Match topics 1–4 with arguments in favor of censorship a–e. There's one extra argument.

   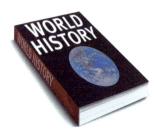

1  sensitive government information
2  Internet sites
3  books
4  history

a ☐ Too many details might erode trust.
b ☐ Too much can make you nervous.
c ☐ The more control, the better.
d ☐ They might be too upsetting.
e ☐ Kids lack the maturity to evaluate them.

**C** In pairs, can you remember Seth's four arguments <u>against</u> censorship? Check in AS 4.13 on p.162 and underline them.

**D** ▶4.14 Match the sentence halves. Listen to check. Which of the highlighted expressions did you know?

1  You should be up front about
2  The truth always comes out when your
3  A company has to hire you
4  We have no need to see
5  I want to know what my government
6  If we conceal information,
7  Shouldn't some novels be banned from

a ☐ sensitive government documents.
b ☐ boss starts to wonder why you're secretive.
c ☐ kids will be suspicious.
d ☐ a prior conviction.
e ☐ with all the information on the table.
f ☐ is up to.
g ☐ school?

### 10 Keep talking

**A** Choose a topic from 9A or B, and decide if you are for or against censorship. Note down at least three arguments to support your position.

**B** **Make it personal** In groups, present your arguments using the expressions below and in 9D. Whose are the most convincing?

> Rarely do we …   That may be, but …   That's my whole point.
> There's no such thing as …   I'm 100% opposed to …   At the very least, it can …

> Schools shouldn't censor what students read. Rarely do kids suffer from overexposure to ideas!

> That may be, but teachers might still have to conceal some information.

♪ (Freedom!) I won't let you down. (Freedom!) I will not give you up

4.5

## 11 Writing: A letter to the editor

**A** Read Julie's letter to the editor. Answer 1–3.
1 Identify the thesis statement in paragraph 1.
2 Identify the opposing argument in paragraph 2.
3 Summarize the main arguments in paragraphs 3–5.

**B** Read *Write it right!* Look at the highlighted expressions (1–7) in context. Then circle the options in 1–4 below that logically reflect Julie's most likely point of view.

### Write it right!
In formal writing, writers support their arguments with fixed expressions that add clarity to their message:
**Contrary to popular belief, I strongly believe that** a job candidate should never be required to reveal a prior conviction.
**There is some debate as to whether** a prior conviction is an accurate predictor of job performance.

1 [**Many would argue that** / **There's certainly no denying that**] "once a criminal, always a criminal."
2 [**There is some debate as to whether** / **I strongly believe that**] personality tests can reveal a criminal mind.
3 [**Irrespective of the seriousness of the crime,** / **There is some debate as to whether**] criminals often serve a lifelong "sentence."
4 [**Despite claims to the contrary,** / **I believe strongly that**] everyone deserves a second chance.

**C Your turn!** Choose a topic from **10B** and write a five to six-paragraph letter to the editor in about 280 words.

**Before**
Decide whether you are for or against, and note down three arguments with supporting details. Also note down an opposing argument.

**While**
Write the letter, following the model. Include expressions from **B** to support your argument in three paragraphs. Introduce your thesis in paragraph 1 and summarize it at the end.

**After**
Post your letter online and read your classmates' work. Whose is most convincing?

### Common mistake
*unemployment*
~~The~~ unemployment also erodes confidence.
Remember: Non-count and plural nouns used to make generalizations have no article.

---

By Julie Montague

Many letters in this column have praised the benefits of openness, transparency, and a lack of censorship. However, there's one area where openness is unlikely to have a positive outcome. ¹I strongly believe that a job candidate should never be required to reveal a prior conviction for a crime. In fact, it should be illegal for employers to gain access to information on crimes that occurred more than 10 years ago.

²Many would argue that employers have a responsibility to their staff, and that safety is of utmost importance. While ³there is certainly no denying that companies need to keep their employees safe, there are compelling reasons to eliminate background checks.

First, ⁴contrary to popular belief, ⁵there is some debate as to whether a prior conviction is an accurate predictor of job performance. The conviction may have been for a minor offense and in an area that has no relevance to the job in question. Moreover, background checks do not provide contextual information or information on mitigating circumstances. They do, however, create an image. And nowhere are our imaginations more active than in imagining the flawed characters of those once convicted of crimes. An enormous pool of potential workers, many of whom have long ago served their sentences, are never given an opportunity to prove their worth. In fact, many never even get so far as an interview.

Second, in no way is public safety undermined more than by having large numbers of unemployed people on the streets. Unemployment also erodes confidence, which, in turn, might encourage a return to crime. Facing a lifetime of social and economic disadvantage, those with prior convictions who cannot find work have little motivation not to fall prey to negative influences. In addition, our economy needs workers willing to take entry-level jobs. ⁶Irrespective of our personal prejudices, employment for all means improvement in our economy, and a rising standard of living across the board actually improves safety.

Finally, ⁷despite claims to the contrary, studies have shown that background checks may contain errors, all of which are a potential tool for discrimination. The information may be out of date, offered by obsolete computer systems. It may not show that an arrest never led to a conviction. And shockingly, even those falsely arrested in cases of mistaken identity may be denied jobs.

For all of the reasons above, I strongly recommend a rethinking of our current policies. Withholding information, as opposed to offering it, may be the best way to offer productive employment to all. Let's not ask a percentage of our population to serve a second, lifetime sentence.

47

# Review 2
## Units 3–4

### 1 Speaking

**A** Look at the photos on p.28.

1 Note down three language-learning techniques you think work well, using these words and expressions.

> access (n,v)   command (n)   get by   improve by leaps and bounds   increase (n,v)
> out of my depth   pick it up   progress (n,v)   put a lot of effort into   rusty

2 In groups, share your reasons. Any original ideas?

> Your vocabulary can improve by leaps and bounds if you listen to music more.

> Really? Have you ever tried that?

**B Make it personal** Language-learning problems!

1 Note down two areas where you're still having trouble. Use participle clauses.

*When speaking to new people, I often feel very shy.*

2 Share your problems with a partner, who will give you advice. Use some of these expressions.

> Problem: I can't even begin to imagine …   I have my doubts about …   to say the least
> … if you ask me   to put it mildly   to a certain extent   so to speak

> Advice: practice makes perfect.   set yourself impossibly high standards   give it a try
> go to the other extreme   hit a middle ground   put your mind to it

> When speaking to new people, I often feel very shy. I have my doubts about whether I seem interesting.

> Maybe you're setting yourself impossibly high standards.

### 2 Grammar

**A** Rewrite Lucille's story about dreams, changing the underlined phrases (1–7) so there is an emphatic inversion using the words in parentheses.

When I woke up in a cold sweat during the night, ¹<u>I didn't know</u> (little) I'd had a fairly common dream. ²<u>When I read an article on the subject, I found out</u> (only when) dreams of being chased were common. ³<u>And they're not only</u> (not only) common, but they usually mean the person is feeling vulnerable. I was feeling that way because I'd broken up with my boyfriend after five years, and ⁴<u>I'd never felt so guilty before</u> (never before). ⁵<u>After I learned that guilt could lead to such dreams, I started to relax</u> (only after) little by little. I'm a lot more aware of my dreams now, and ⁶<u>I haven't had a similar dream since then</u> (not since). Before this happened, ⁷<u>I hardly ever thought</u> (rarely) about the significance of dreams, but now I'm fascinated by the topic.

**B Make it personal** In pairs, share a story about something you learned about yourself from a dream. Use emphatic inversion and formal relative clauses.

> Rarely had I had recurring dreams until I changed schools …

48

## 3 Reading

**A** Read the article about Martin Luther King, Jr. In pairs, recall three reasons he was a great public speaker.

> One of the greatest orators of all time was Martin Luther King, Jr. Only 34 years old when he delivered his famous "I have a dream" speech in 1963, he changed the course of history. However, rarely have people stopped to consider the qualities that made King such a powerful speaker. Let me point out just a few.
>
> First, really convincing speakers are authentic. They have a message to deliver, which they themselves fully embody, and King's life and words were harmonious. By the time he delivered his famous speech, he had already established himself as a committed civil rights leader.
>
> Listen carefully, and you'll also notice King's tone and cadence. He usually began his speeches slowly before building up to a powerful, more rapid delivery. As he increased his pace and volume, he captivated his listeners. Not only did he create a powerful connection in this way, but he also reinforced his message through repetition. The repetition of the words "I have a dream" comes through again and again in his speech.
>
> Finally, while King may have improvised his famous speech, delivered without notes, what is less well-known is that not only had he been practicing parts of it for years, he also had been preaching about dreams since 1960. Rehearsing his message over and over, King was able to evaluate its impact on smaller audiences to whom he had delivered it. Fully aware that "practice makes perfect," he honed his talents. It is no wonder that "I have a dream" was ranked the top speech of the 20th century in a 1999 poll.

**B Make it personal** 🌐 Search on "I have a dream," and read or listen to the speech. What other qualities do you feel make a good public speaker?

> He mentions history a lot, so listeners can feel part of something greater.

## 4 Self-test

Correct the two mistakes in each sentence. Check your answers in Units 3 and 4. What's your score, 1–20?

1. I used to feel really out of the depth at college, even though I could more or less get through.
2. You're putting yourself very high standards and need to hit a middle road.
3. Why do I still have an accent is a mystery, but an article I read recently said speaking makes perfect.
4. How often people uses hashtags differ from one location to another.
5. At first, I couldn't get the word in edgewise, but later on, I was actually at a loss for the words.
6. I wouldn't go too far as to say it's an age-related illness.
7. Not only I watched the guy break in to the apartment, but I also tipped up the cops.
8. It's the movie which the show is based and about that I wrote a review.
9. So many people suffer from stress-oriented problems, most of who don't know it.
10. I read lots of blogs from that I get ideas, unrespective of the author.

## 5 Point of view

Choose a topic. Then support your opinion in 100–150 words, and record your answer. Ask a partner for feedback. How can you be more convincing?

a. You feel most people have serious hidden biases. OR
   You feel only a small percentage do, just like a small percentage believes in conspiracy theories.

b. You think parents need to monitor what their children read. OR
   You think any kind of censorship is inappropriate and kids need to be exposed to the real world.

# 5 » Why do good plans sometimes fail?

## 1 Listening

**A** ▶5.1 In pairs, use the photo and excerpts from a radio show (1–4) about a publicity stunt to guess what happened. Listen to check. How close were you?

1. Snapple sought to break a world record, so it came up with a creative if crazy idea: erect the world's largest popsicle.
2. It was roughly 80 degrees outside.
3. They're usually very thorough when planning big campaigns.
4. Sounds as chaotic as a snowstorm with unploughed side streets!

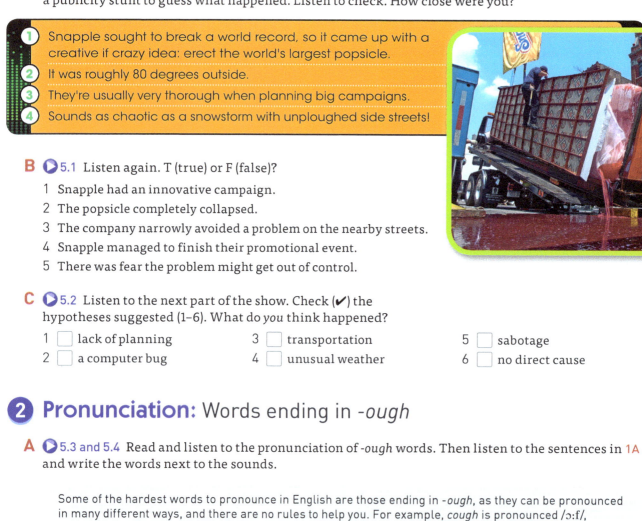

**B** ▶5.1 Listen again. T (true) or F (false)?
1. Snapple had an innovative campaign.
2. The popsicle completely collapsed.
3. The company narrowly avoided a problem on the nearby streets.
4. Snapple managed to finish their promotional event.
5. There was fear the problem might get out of control.

**C** ▶5.2 Listen to the next part of the show. Check (✔) the hypotheses suggested (1–6). What do *you* think happened?

1. ☐ lack of planning
2. ☐ a computer bug
3. ☐ transportation
4. ☐ unusual weather
5. ☐ sabotage
6. ☐ no direct cause

## 2 Pronunciation: Words ending in -ough

**A** ▶5.3 and 5.4 Read and listen to the pronunciation of *-ough* words. Then listen to the sentences in **1A** and write the words next to the sounds.

> Some of the hardest words to pronounce in English are those ending in *-ough*, as they can be pronounced in many different ways, and there are no rules to help you. For example, *cough* is pronounced /ɔ:f/, whereas *tough* is pronounced /ʌf/, and *through* is pronounced /u:/.
>
> a /oʊ/ (al)though _____    c /ʌf/ enough _____
> b /ɔ:/ thought _____    d /aʊ/ drought _____

**B** 🌐 **Make it personal** Search online for other "publicity disasters." In groups, share the most interesting stories. Use the sentences below. Pronounce the underlined words correctly.

| [Company] <u>sought</u> to _____ , but it didn't work. |
| They must have _____ <u>thoroughly</u>, but it was a fiasco. |
| Things got a bit (really) <u>rough</u> when _____ . |
| It must have been <u>tough</u> for them (not) to _____ . |

> Here's one. A U.S. company sought to prove it offered identity-theft protection and posted the CEO's personal information. Can you believe it?

> Was he hacked?

> He sure was! And things got really rough when he was also fined for deceptive advertising!

♪ Yeah, I know that I let you down. Is it too late to say I'm sorry now?

5.1

## 3 Vocabulary: Failed plans

**A** ▶5.5 Match the two sentence halves. Listen to check.

1. They were **on the verge of** something big,
2. Their plans **fell through** and the whole thing
3. The company decided to **call** the whole thing **off**
4. But was it an **oversight**?
5. It was a **high-stakes** operation, meaning that
6. It might have been a **glitch** or something, maybe

a ☐ and stopped raising the popsicle.
b ☐ but the campaign never materialized.
c ☐ if it failed, it would be a disaster.
d ☐ ended in a sticky mess.
e ☐ I mean, didn't they see it coming?
f ☐ software related.

**B** Choose the most likely meaning (a or b) for the **highlighted** expressions (1–6) in **A**.

1  a ☐ about to experience something          b ☐ at the end of a difficult process
2  a ☐ took a long time to succeed            b ☐ failed
3  a ☐ cancel                                 b ☐ delay
4  a ☐ a deliberate mistake                   b ☐ an unanticipated mistake
5  a ☐ important and risky                    b ☐ important and relatively risk-free
6  a ☐ an unexpected, but minor problem       b ☐ a lack of attention to detail

**C** In pairs, role-play retelling the popsicle fiasco as: 1) a journalist reporting it on TV or 2) the owner of Snapple talking to the campaign planner. Use the new expressions in **A**.

> Snapple planned a really high-stakes promotion event, and …

**D** ▶5.6 Listen to the DJ's story and take notes. Then summarize it using expressions from **A**.

**E Make it personal** Can you remember a plan or goal that fell through?

1 ▶5.7 **How to say it** Complete the chart. Listen to check.

| Talking about disappointments |  |
|---|---|
| What they said | What they meant |
| 1  I fell flat on my _____. | I failed completely. |
| 2  Things got out of _____. | Things got out of control. |
| 3  It took me a while to _____ myself together. | It took me a while to recover. |
| 4  It was _____ to square one! | I had to start from scratch. |
| 5  I came this _____ to (having a nervous breakdown)! | I almost (had a nervous breakdown). |

2 Choose a topic and note down a few details. Ask yourself:
   *What / When / Where / Why / How …?*

   a date     a do-it-yourself project     a job application     a party     travel plans

3 In pairs, share your stories. Use expressions from **A** and **E**. Any comic moments?

> I once invited 20 people to a party and at the last minute, I dropped all the food on the floor.

> You're kidding!

> I came this close to having a nervous breakdown. I wasn't sure whether to call the whole thing off …

**Common mistake**
*losing*
I came close to ~~lose~~ my job.

51

## 5.2 Do you ever make resolutions?

### 4 Language in use

**A** ▶ 5.8 Listen to the start of a documentary about New Year's resolutions. Which of the man's resolutions isn't mentioned? How many other resolutions can you list in one minute?

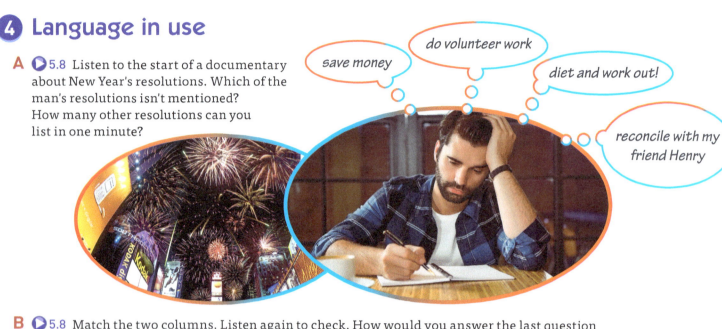

**B** ▶ 5.8 Match the two columns. Listen again to check. How would you answer the last question the reporter asks?

| Making resolutions | | Keeping resolutions | |
|---|---|---|---|
| 1 make | ☐ anew | 4 get | ☐ with your (plans) |
| 2 start | ☐ a fresh start | 5 follow through | ☐ your act together |
| 3 turn | ☐ the page | 6 stick to | ☐ your (resolutions) |

> I think the reason is that we have too many temptations.

**C** ▶ 5.9 Listen to the second part. Choose the answer (a or b) that matches the doctor's opinion. Any surprising information?

1 "Given what we know about the nature of the human psyche, this shouldn't come as a surprise."
   Why not?
   a ☐ Our habits may have emotional origins.   b ☐ Willpower is a relatively rare quality.

2 "With a view to better understanding the problem, a number of researchers have looked at the success rates of peoples' resolutions."
   What were the results?
   a ☐ They tend to reveal a recurring pattern.   b ☐ They vary widely from person to person.

3 "So you're saying some people sabotage themselves so as not to succeed?"
   How do they do that?
   a ☐ By making too many resolutions.   b ☐ By setting the bar too high.

4 "But in view of what we know about recent motivational theories, this rarely works."
   What are they talking about?
   a ☐ Focusing on small steps.   b ☐ Focusing on the end result.

**D Make it personal** Look at your list of New Year's Resolutions from A. Answer 1–4 using expressions from B. Which resolutions (if any) ...

1 have you made in recent years?
2 were you / would you be able to stick to? For how long?
3 would you consider making this coming December 31?
4 might have / have had the biggest impact on your life?

> I had terrible eating habits, so last year, I decided to get my act together.

> Good for you! Were you able to stick to your new plan?

52

♪ All is quiet on New Year's Day. A world in white gets underway. I want to be with you, Be with you night and day

5.2

## 5 Grammar: Formal conjunctions and prepositions

**A** Read the grammar box and complete rules 1–3. Then rephrase the quotes in 4C using *to* or *because of*.

| Formal conjunctions and prepositions for reason and purpose | | |
|---|---|---|
| In view of<br>Given<br>Thanks to | the increase in stress levels,<br>the fact that life is so busy,<br>good promotion, | more and more people are doing yoga. |
| With the aim of<br>With a view to | studying people's resolutions, | a number of studies were conducted. |
| So as to<br>In an effort to | save money, | I moved back in with my parents. |
| 1 _____ , _____ , and _____ mean "because of." | | |
| 2 _____ , _____ , _____ , and _____ mean "(in order) to." | | |
| 3 *With a view to* is followed by the _____ form. *So as to* is followed by the _____ form. | | |

» Grammar expansion p.146

**B** Read the blog post and circle the correct alternatives (1–5).

### Resolutions, goals, deadlines ...

¹[**Given** / **With a view to**] our hectic lifestyles, our days sometimes pass us by while our minds are elsewhere, either dwelling in the past or making plans. I work for a major finance company and ²[**with the aim of** / **in view of**] the long hours I had to work, I kept trying new relaxation techniques ³[**so as to** / **with a view to**] reduce the toll on my physical and mental well-being. That was when a friend suggested mindfulness, and it's changed my life. Mindfulness means being aware of your senses, actions, and thoughts. It's living in the present moment ⁴[**with the aim of** / **thanks to**] feeling more relaxed and fulfilled. I started to practice it throughout the day ⁵[**with a view to** / **in an effort to**] defeat anxiety, and I couldn't be happier.

**C** Rephrase 1–5 using the words in parentheses.

So ... Why do we live in the future? ¹We live in the future because it offers endless possibilities. (in view of) ²We feel dissatisfied in the present, so we take refuge in the future. (given) ³We fantasize about our future successes because we want to escape our current misery. (in an effort to) How can we live in the present moment? ⁴Accept the fact that there are things you can't control if you want to find peace. (so as to) ⁵Learn how to do one thing at a time so that you can give it your full attention. (with a view to)

### Common mistake

*in view of the fact that / given (the fact that)*
I decided to resign ~~in view of~~ there were no fringe benefits.

"the fact that" is optional after *given*, but obligatory after *in view of*.

**D** **Make it personal** Are we in control of our destiny?

1 Explain the idea behind each quote (a–f). Use some of the formal conjunctions and prepositions in A.

  a "Life is what happens to you while you're busy making other plans." (performed by John Lennon; attributed to Allen Saunders)
  b "There's so much to be said for challenging fate instead of ducking behind it." (Diana Trilling)
  c "Maybe our mistakes are what make our fate." (Sarah Jessica Parker)
  d "I think in terms of the day's resolutions, not the year's." (Henry Moore)
  e "Our history is not our destiny." (Alan Cohen)
  f "I think destiny is just a fancy word for a psychological problem." (Jodie Foster)

2 Choose your favorite one. Why do you like it?

> I think the last one means that given that people keep repeating the same patterns, their destiny may actually be some sort of emotional problem.

53

## 5.3 How well do you deal with failure?

### 6 Reading

**A** Read the introduction. In one minute, list all the parts of life people commonly fail at that you can think of. Then in pairs, suggest an answer for the last question.

> Well, for one thing, most people fail in their relationships from time to time ...

# Coming to terms with failure

Can you think of even one person who doesn't dread failure and go to great lengths to avoid it? Who in their right mind would want to experience all the negative emotions that come from failing to accomplish an important goal? Obviously the answer is no one. However, failure is an inherent part of life, so our best bet is to keep it in perspective. Why is that so very difficult?

"Well, there's nowhere to go but up."

**Below are five strategies designed to help you make it through unscathed:**

1 **Be upset!** Yes, that's right. Give in to your emotions. Simultaneously, reject the temptation to take failure personally. Even though your relationship or job didn't pan out, you are still a successful person. Separate your failure from your self-esteem. You'll go far. And the proof: Lady Gaga was fired from her record label after only three months. Ang Lee failed Taiwan's college entrance examinations and couldn't get into acting because his English "wasn't good enough." Look where they are today. Lady Gaga may have "cried so hard she couldn't talk," but we know she succeeded in putting her failure behind her.

2 **Snap out of it!** After you've had a good cry, then it's time to move on. The longer you dwell on your failure, the more miserable you'll be. The Irish writer Oscar Wilde died young and faced many obstacles in his lifetime. But you'd do well to heed his advice, "Life is too important a thing ever to talk seriously about." It's critical not to obsess about what might have been because you'll only sink deeper into depression.

3 **Make a right turn.** Think of your failure as you would a road blocked by construction and evaluate it logically. First you take stock of the situation, and then you act. And fairly quickly. The same can be said for failure. You need to keep moving, but just in a slightly different direction. Oh, "come on," you might say. That analogy doesn't hold water. The evidence, however, shows it does. A case in point is Theodore Seuss Geisel, known as Dr. Seuss – author of *The cat in the hat* and many other children's books that have delighted young readers the world over. He had his first book rejected by 27 publishers! Just as he was on the verge of burning the manuscript, he ran into an old classmate who helped him get it published at Vanguard Press. You may not know that until this point, Geisel had supported himself entirely through drawing cartoons.

4 **Reject others' opinions.** If you hold on to someone else's negative opinion of you, it will be hard to move forward, so be careful to avoid that trap! Never forget that what someone thinks is true about you may actually be false. Terry Gross of National Public Radio felt she "couldn't do anything" when she failed at her first teaching job and was fired after only six weeks. That was before she discovered radio. Her program "Fresh Air" now reaches over five million listeners.

5 **Focus on the positive!** It may seem obvious, but your attitude may be the only thing separating you from those who have achieved greatness. It's so tempting to let a negative voice take over, and give way to anger and despair. However, Confucius certainly had it right when he proclaimed, "Our greatest glory is not in never falling, but in rising every time we fall."

♪ When you try your best, but you don't succeed. When you get what you want, but not what you need

## 5.3

**B** ▶ 5.10 Listen to and read the whole article. In pairs, complete each sentence so that it captures the essence of each section in the article.
1 Even if you've failed, it's OK to be upset, but important not to ___take failure personally___.
2 Stop obsessing about your failure because _____.
3 Look at failure analytically, which means _____.
4 It's dangerous to give too much power to others' opinions because _____.
5 It's important to think positively and _____.

**C** Find the underlined words in the article. Circle the word or expression with the same meaning in context.
1 dread: [**feel afraid of** / **feel reluctant about**] failure
2 unscathed: [**uninjured physically** / **unharmed emotionally**]
3 give in to: [**accept** / **hand over**]
4 pan out: [**succeed** / **take place**]
5 heed: [**read** / **pay attention to**]
6 hold water: [**seem factual** / **seem logical**]

**D Make it personal** Choose a statement from B you agree with. Do you have a story to back it up?

> I totally agree with number 1. Let me tell you about what happened to me at my old school ...

## 7 Vocabulary: Evaluating success

**A** Complete 1–6 with six of the <mark>highlighted</mark> expressions from the article. What's your favorite tip? Can you think of any others?

### Success: Don't let it go to your head!

Some people ¹_____ to achieve success in life, but don't always know what to do with it. Here are four tips to help you ²_____ fame and fortune _____.

– Keep your feet on the ground. Before making major decisions, stop and ³_____ of your values, goals, and interests.
– Fame doesn't erase your own failures, so be empathetic! You've just ⁴_____ them _____ you successfully and moved on.
– Keep in mind that success may not last forever, however hard you may try to ⁵_____ it.
– If you find your new-found fortune slips away, there's no point ⁶_____ what might have been. Remember, you're still you!

**B Make it personal** In pairs, discuss 1–2.
1 Do you know anyone who changed after he / she got ...

a new job    famous    into college    married    promoted    rich

2 What happened? Use expressions from A.

> My brother went to great lengths to find a new job. But then ...

## 5.4 Have you ever had a wrong first impression?

### 8 Language in use

**A** ▶5.11 Listen and match six conversations to pictures a–f. In pairs, what character trait was the surprise in each case?

> In the first one, the guy was actually irresponsible.

**B** ▶5.12 Read the conversation excerpts and guess whether the speakers are those in A or new people. Listen to check.

1. I resent him expecting me to do everything! I thought I could **count on** his help, but I can't. It looks as if I'll have to **team up with** someone else.

2. I heard about you breaking up and that you couldn't **work** things **out**. I can see why you didn't want to stay with him!

3. Bill and I have some legitimate concerns about your not **sticking to** the deadline. I know that might strike you as heartless.

4. The principal is appalled at the boy's cheating and plans to **take** the matter **up** with his parents.

5. She appreciated us inviting her, even though it didn't **come off** that way ... We might **wind up** being good friends.

6. The police officer insisted on our coming to the station. At first, I thought he'd **let** us **off**.

**C** ▶5.12 Listen again. Complete the misleading behaviors. Which one is the worst?
1. Roger misled Barbara by taking _____ and asking _____.
2. At first John would ask about Ann's _____ and cook a wonderful _____.
3. Bill used to stop by Susan's _____ often and ask about her _____.
4. Simon would talk about _____ and _____ in classes on social issues.
5. Georgina didn't know Amy was _____ because she always offered to give _____.
6. The officer had good _____ and a _____ accent.

> **Common mistake**
> I'm really counting ~~with~~ *on* you.

**D** Write the highlighted phrasal verbs in B next to their meanings in context.
1. _____ solve
2. _____ depend on
3. _____ not punish
4. _____ work with
5. _____ stay with
6. _____ end up
7. _____ discuss
8. _____ seem, appear

**E** Make it personal  Has your first impression of anyone ever been really wrong? How did you find out? Share your stories in groups, using phrasal verbs from C. Whose was the most unusual?

> I had a neighbor who came off as really easygoing at first. He smiled a lot and told jokes. But then one day, he showed his true colors!

♪ You and I should ride the coast and wind up in our favorite coats just miles away

5.4

## 9 Grammar: Nouns, object pronouns, and possessive adjectives + -ing form

**A** Read the grammar box and check (✔) the correct rules.

| Levels of formality in nouns, object pronouns, and possessive adjectives + -ing form |||||
|---|---|---|---|
| Informal | I'm sick of | **my mom** | yelling at me. |
| | Roger was counting on | **me** | helping him with the project. |
| | I resent | **you** | not doing your fair share. |
| | The officer insisted on | **them** | going to the station. |
| Neutral to formal | I'm against | **our school's** | giving so many exams. |
| | My boss showed concern about | **my** | not turning in the report. |
| | He wasn't very supportive of | **your** | being sick. |
| | I'm uncomfortable with | **their** | not giving me an honest answer. |

1 Informal sentences have a(n) ☐ **object pronoun** ☐ **possessive adjective** before the verb, and more formal sentences have a(n) ☐ **object pronoun** ☐ **possessive adjective.**
2 Therefore, when talking to your boss, say "I appreciate ☐ **him** ☐ **his** calling me" because it is ☐ **more** ☐ **less** formal.
3 The form of the verb is ☐ **sometimes** ☐ **always** an -ing form, and the form of the negative is ☐ **sometimes** ☐ **always** not.
4 When there is a noun before a verb, the more formal form is ☐ **possessive** ☐ **plural**.

**Grammar expansion p.146**

**B** Find the six undelined examples in **8B** of nouns, pronouns, or possessive adjectives before -ing forms. Write I next to the informal forms and N next to the neutral to formal ones.

**C** Rewrite 1–7 informally with nouns or object pronouns. Do you identify with any of the complaints? Can you think of any others?

### Top seven relationship complaints
1 "She's constantly criticizing me. I'm tired of that."
2 "His parents drop by unexpectedly. I'm not comfortable with that."
3 "You snore. I'm tired of that."
4 "Jim is Facebook friends with his ex. I resent that."
5 "He gives me the silent treatment when he's angry. I'll never get used to that."
6 "I take a long time to answer his texts. He can't stand that."
7 "We want different things. I'm not happy with that."

*I'm tired of her constantly criticizing me.*

**D Make it personal** Do you approve? In groups, read the headlines and share your reactions. Use nouns or object pronouns before -ing forms, where possible. Any big differences?

I'm (not) in favor of ...   I'm against ...   I'm concerned about ...   I'm skeptical of ...

1 **A bittersweet ending: Japanese train station closes after lone passenger, picked up every day at 7:04 a.m. and brought back at 5:08 p.m., graduates from high school**
2 **Undercover officer dressed as homeless man catches drivers using phones**
3 **Vice-principal greets students with singing, dancing every morning**
4 **Table manners rewarded: restaurant offers diners 5% off to drop their devices**

> I'm not in favor of trains operating with just one passenger. What a waste of money!

> I disagree. This station stayed open to support education.

57

## 5.5 How bad are drivers where you live?

### 10 Listening

**A** ▶5.13 Listen to a conversation between Monica and Ed about bad drivers. In pairs, answer 1–2.
1 What dangers do pedestrians face in their city?
2 What does Ed think can be done about it?

**B** ▶5.14 Listen to a second conversation. Note down …
1 two problems with Ed's proposal for a test based on the London exam.
2 one problem with Monica's proposal for speed bumps.

**C** ▶5.15 Listen to a third conversation. Check (✔) the aspects of driver psychology mentioned.
1 ☐ future ability to stay focused   2 ☐ driver sociability   3 ☐ current degree of concentration

**D** **Make it personal** In pairs, would Monica and Ed's proposal work in your city? Is the revised proposal an improvement?

> I think it's still impractical. What if a driver can only afford one driving test?

### 11 Keep talking

**A** ▶5.16 Read *Proposal language*. Then complete 1–5 using a form of the words or expressions in the box. There's one extra. Listen to check.

> **Proposal language**
>
> Specific expressions are used to talk about proposals. For example, we *make* or *put together* a proposal, and a proposal has a *rationale* behind it, or central reason for existing.

| airtight   entail   put together   rationale   redo   spell out   steps   turn down |
|---|

1 I'm going to _____ a proposal anyway. And maybe I can submit it next week.
2 They _____ my proposal. Guess it's back to square 1.
3 What did your proposal _____ ? What was the general idea?
4 The _____ was that there would be a special exam for city drivers.
5 It [the proposal]'s got to be _____ this time. It has to _____ all the different _____ and show how to get from point A to point B.

**B** In groups, choose a topic below and develop a proposal. Make certain it has a clear rationale and list at least four features as bullet points. Use proposal language from A and the expressions below. Share it with the class. Whose is most convincing?

How to …

evaluate students who aren't good at exams   develop new parking rules in your city
make your neighborhood cleaner or safer   offer scholarships to needy students
earn money if you can't find a good job

| I think you're on to something.   Why not focus on …?   Suppose you only …   You've got a point. |
|---|

> OK, exams. My proposal is to eliminate the final exam.

> I think you're on to something. First, let's go over the rationale.

♪ It's all over the front page. You give me road rage

5.5

## 12 Writing: A proposal

**A** Read the proposal and find ...
1. the purpose of the email.
2. one supporting argument for each of the goals in paragraphs 4, 5, and 6.
3. the next step in the proposal.

**B** Read *Write it right!* Then read 1–4 and choose the most logical answers.

> **Write it right!**
>
> In many kinds of writing, adverbs and adverbial expressions not only help to link ideas, but they also signal what the sentence or next point will be about:
>
> **Admittedly** [= I concede it's true that] our school is not a charity.

1. [**Admittedly** / **Incidentally**] we have an ambitious plan, but we still think there are ways to achieve it.
2. [**Frankly** / **Essentially**], our proposal can be summarized in one sentence.
3. [**Apparently** / **Obviously**], it seems two other schools have tried something similar from what I've heard.
4. [**Obviously** / **Broadly speaking**], our proposal has three parts.

**C** Read *Formulaic expressions (1)*. Circle five more fixed expressions in the underlined sentences in the proposal.

> **Formulaic expressions (1)**
>
> Formal letters and emails often contain formulaic expressions, where the wording is fixed. They facilitate written communication by offering standard openings, closings, and other useful language.
>
> Thank you (very much) for your response to our proposal of February 15 (date).

**D** **Your turn!** Choose a proposal you discussed in **11B** and write a formal email to present it in about 280 words.

**Before**
Plan three arguments for your proposal and note down supporting details.

**While**
Write five to six paragraphs to support your proposal, following the model in **A**. Use a variety of adverbs and at least one formulaic sentence.

**After**
Post your essay online and read your classmates' work. Whose proposal is most convincing?

---

Dear Ms. Harbinger:

Thank you very much for your response to our proposal of February 15. We were quite disappointed that our project wasn't accepted, as I'm sure you can understand. However, we understand that the budget was insufficient. With the aim of finding an acceptable solution, we've rethought some aspects of our strategy. I'd now like to propose the following in an effort to submit a plan that is more practical:

1. Our school would offer a scholarship each semester to 50 qualifying students, rather than a full scholarship.
2. The remaining tuition costs would be covered in three potential ways:
   a) Through work-study programs at our school.
   b) By offering loans, which would be repaid within ten years of graduation.
   c) By offering part-time degree programs, thereby allowing students to pay half tuition and take jobs in the community.

**Broadly speaking**, we have three goals: (1) to give needy students a chance at upward mobility, (2) to expand our student base and make it more diverse, and most importantly, (3) to reward academic effort and achievement. The importance of these objectives cannot be overemphasized, so please allow me to elaborate.

**Admittedly**, our school is not a charity. Nevertheless, our long-term goal should be a more egalitarian society with opportunities for all. **Frankly**, in the 21st century, with the acute needs of our global economy at stake, we simply cannot afford to have segments of society who are left without access to continuing education. Upward mobility must be a dream within the reach of all of us.

Exposing students to diversity is also important if we hope to create a society free of conflict, and **essentially**, our school has attracted students from only one social and economic background. Apparently, as we've learned from a survey we conducted in one of the communities we have in mind, promotion is not reaching students from across the city. In view of this, we feel we need to try harder. We owe it to our students to enable them to experience the richness of different cultures and sub-cultures. **Incidentally**, a brief survey here at Fourth District College shows that our own students find this goal important, as well.

**Clearly**, in a just society, academic achievement must be rewarded also. Poor students, quite **obviously**, face enough obstacles and prejudice. This last goal doesn't seem to require amplification.

I hope I have managed to provide a convincing rationale. Regarding our next step, we would be happy to meet with you at your convenience to discuss the specifics. We will do our best to answer any questions you may have.

Sincerely,
Ricardo Ortega
Student Council President

59

# 6

## Do you still read paper books?

### 1 Listening

**A** ▶6.1 Listen to the start of an interview with Dr. Soars. Then in pairs, look at photos 1–2 and compare your understanding of "the digital apocalypse never came."

**B** ▶6.2 Guess whether the features (1–6) are E (e-book), P (paper book), or NI (no information)? Listen to the next part to check.

1 convenient
2 affordable
3 prone to damage
4 environmentally friendly
5 sensory-rich
6 reader friendly

**C** ▶6.2 Listen again. Match the opinions (1–6) to their responses (a–e). Then give your own responses.

1 Paper books aren't going anywhere in the foreseeable future.
2 Reading is essentially an abstract activity, right?
3 You see, reading involves a certain degree of physicality.
4 So … e-books fail to recreate this sort of hands-on experience?
5 Some people find it easier to take notes using a pen or pencil.

a ☐ "You've lost me there."
b ☐ "But how can that be?"
c ☐ "Well, guilty as charged."
d ☐ "Well, yes and no."
e ☐ "To some extent, yes."

> Paper books aren't going anywhere in the foreseeable future.

> I completely disagree. Actually, I just read today that …

**D** ▶6.3 Listen to the end of the interview. How does Dr. Soars feel about phone reading? Do you agree?

**E** ▶6.3 Match the two columns. Listen again to check. Which phrases do you associate with fast reading?

| 1 skip | a ☐ it past the first paragraph |
| 2 (not) make | b ☐ your eyes over a text |
| 3 run | c ☐ over whole sentences |

| 4 get | a ☐ over a challenging text |
| 5 pore | b ☐ the gist of a text |
| 6 read | c ☐ between the lines |

**F Make it personal** In groups, discuss 1–2.

1 Do you think paper books will have a future similar to CDs? Why (not)?
2 How do you usually read these items? Use expressions from **E**.

books by (Stephen King)   (Facebook) posts   (computer) instruction manuals
news about (politics)   (physics) textbooks   (rental) contracts

> I almost always read Facebook posts on my phone. They're usually short, so I can get the gist right away.

> I like to read them on my laptop so I don't just skip over the comments.

♪ I got a shelf full of books and most of my teeth. A few pairs of socks and a door with a lock

**6.1**

## 2 Vocabulary: Phrasal verbs with *out*

**A** ▶ 6.4 Complete 1–6 with the nouns in the box. Listen to check.

> e-books   meaning   nature   sentences   studies   titles

1 It's so much easier to browse an online store, **pick out** (= select from a group) your favorite _____ and download them.
2 You can't **wear out** (= damage from too much use) or accidentally tear _____ .
3 A paper book has an easily indentifiable size, shape, and weight, which **brings out** (= reveals) its more concrete _____ .
4 Some people find it easier to take notes, highlight, or even **cross out** (= draw a line through) _____ in a paper book.
5 Some _____ **point out** (= mention) that people reading on their phones take lots of shortcuts.
6 They're also more likely to ignore unknown words rather than **work out** (= try to discover) their _____ in context or look them up.

**B** Complete the mind maps with highlighted phrasal verbs from A. Then, in pairs, use the prompts to find out more about each other.

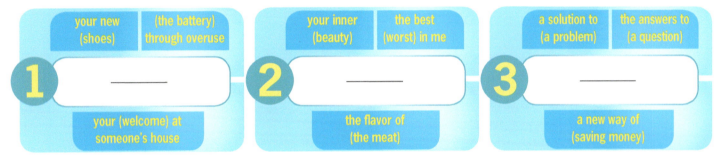

> Do / Have you ever …?   When did you last …?   Who in your (family) …?   What do you do to / when …?
> What's the best way to …?   What would you do if …?

> Have you ever … your welcome at someone's house?

> Not as far as I know! I hope not.

**C Make it personal** How do you feel about reading?

1 Choose your three favorite quotes from those below. In pairs, explain what they mean.

a "'Classic' — a book which people praise and don't read." (Mark Twain)
b "Think before you speak. Read before you think." (Fran Lebowitz)
c "Books are no more threatened by Kindle than stairs by elevators." (Stephen Fry)
d "School made us 'literate' but did not teach us to read for pleasure." (Ambeth R. Ocampo)
e "No two persons ever read the same book." (Edmund Wilson)
f "Today a reader, tomorrow a leader." (Margaret Fuller)
g "Read a thousand books, and your words will flow like a river." (Lisa See)
h "If you don't like to read, you haven't found the right book." (J.K. Rowling)

> I really like b. The first part is pretty obvious. But the second part means that books help us think in new ways. They bring out our creativity.

2 Do the quotes remind you of anyone or anything? Share your ideas, using phrasal verbs from A where possible.

61

## 6.2 Do you ever watch dubbed movies?

### 3 Language in use

**A** ▶6.5 Listen to two friends, Grace and Noah, talking about the movie *La Vie en Rose*. Complete 1–5 with short phrases.

1 Grace really enjoyed watching the movie, while Noah _____ .
2 He's not used to _____ .
3 In Germany, most TV shows and movies _____ .
4 Grace seems surprised, given _____ .
5 Countries that avoid subtitles include _____ .

**B** ▶6.6 Guess the speaker's main arguments. Then listen to check. Can you think of any others?

Noah doesn't like subtitles because …
1 he misses _____ .
2 it's hard for him not to _____ .

Grace doesn't like dubbed movies because …
3 the voices don't _____ .
4 actors can't _____ as well.

**C** ▶6.7 Read *Using out of*. Then write the use of *out of* (1–4) next to the bold phrases below. Listen to check. Notice the /ə/ sound in *of*.

> **Using *out of***
>
> *Out of* is a very common prepositional phrase. Here are four uses:
> 1 movement from within outwards: *We walked **out of the room**.*
> 2 caused or motivated by: *I watched the Oscars last night, more **out of curiosity** than interest.*
> 3 not having: *The theater company is **out of money** and can't produce a new play this year. Lots of record stores went **out of business** in the 2010s.*
> 4 selection from a group: *Ask anyone who the greatest American actress is, and at least **three out of five** people will say Meryl Streep.*

1 In Germany, nearly every foreign TV show is dubbed. I mean, like **8 out of 10** ☐, unless it's pay per view or something.
2 I end up reading the subtitles whether or not I understand what's being said. I guess I do it **out of** sheer **habit** ☐ – just in case I might have missed something.
3 It annoys me how the actors' lips and their voices are always a little **out of sync** ☐, even if the dubbing is done well.
4 Sometimes I just feel like getting up and walking **out of the theater** ☐.
5 I don't mind the occasional subtitle as long as there's not too much text to process. Otherwise, I find I'm **out of patience** ☐ pretty quickly.

**D Make it personal** In groups, answer 1–3.

1 Modify 1–5 in **C** so that they're true for you.
2 Are most foreign movies dubbed or subtitled where you live?
3 🌐 Search on a recent movie in English that you've seen or would like to see and watch the original trailer (name of movie + "original trailer"). Then search again for a dubbed trailer in your own language (name of movie in your language + "trailer" + name of language) and compare.

> I just watched the trailer for the movie *Brooklyn* in English and Spanish. I couldn't stand the dubbed version!

> What was wrong with it?

> Well, for one thing, the accents, one of the most appealing parts of the movie, were completely lost. The Irish accent, the Italian-American accent: they're all gone!

♪ I'm out of touch, I'm out of luck, I'll pick you up when you're getting down

6.2

## 4 Grammar: Adverb clauses of condition

**A** Read the grammar box and check (✔) the correct rules (1–2). Do 1–5 below mean the same as a–e? Write S (same) or D (different).

| Adverb clauses of condition: as long as, whether or not, in case, unless, and even if ||
|---|---|
| a I don't mind dubbed films | **as long as** the voices are good. |
| b **Whether or not** you speak Spanish, | you should try to watch the original versions. |
| c I think I should turn on the subtitles | **in case** I miss something. |
| d **Unless** I stop watching dubbed movies, | my listening won't improve. |
| e I don't miss a single episode of The Simpsons | **even if** it's the dubbed version. |

1 In the clause expressing condition, the verb is always in the ☐ **present** ☐ **future**.
2 We ☐ **use** ☐ **don't use** a comma when the main clause comes first.

Remember: *Even though* expresses contrast, not condition:
**Even though** I don't like Quentin Tarantino that much, I enjoyed his latest movie.
I rarely watch Hollywood blockbusters, **even if** the reviews are good.

» Grammar expansion p.148

1 I don't object to dubbed films, but only if the voices are good.
2 You should try to watch the original versions, especially if you speak Spanish.
3 There's a chance I might miss something. I think I ought to turn on the subtitles.
4 My listening won't get better if I don't stop watching dubbed movies.
5 I don't watch The Simpsons if it's dubbed.

**Common mistake**
We're going away for the weekend ~~even though~~ *even if* it rains. Nothing's going to stop us!

**B** Circle the correct answers. Can you think of any other reasons?

### Three reasons people aren't going to the movies anymore

1 **Ticket prices**
Ticket prices are on the rise, especially now with IMAX and 3D. This might put some viewers off, ¹[**as long as** / **unless**] they have the extra money to spare, of course. Not to mention the popcorn, which we're mysteriously compelled to buy, ²[**even if** / **whether or not**] we're actually hungry!

2 **Streaming**
Who needs to leave home on Saturday night when there's Netflix? ³[**As long as** / **Even if**] you have an Internet connection – ⁴[**even if** / **even though**] it's a relatively slow one – you can watch thousands of movies from the comfort of your couch.

3 **Better quality TV**
⁵[**In case** / **Unless**] you haven't noticed, we might be experiencing the golden age of television. Because of shows such as Game of Thrones, people don't need to go to the movies anymore.

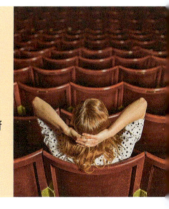

**C Make it personal** In groups, discuss which trends are popular.

1 Among people your age, are more or fewer people doing these things compared to five years ago? Write M (more) or F (fewer).

| Arts, news, and entertainment | Shopping | Relationships |
|---|---|---|
| reading paper newspapers | buying bigger cars | sticking to relationships |
| going to museums / galleries | avoiding brand names | interacting face to face |
| downloading / streaming music | choosing more casual clothes | breaking up by text message |

2 Choose two trends. Give three reasons that might explain each one. Use expressions from A and 3C.

> More people my age are definitely breaking up by text message unless they were very serious.

> How awful! Why do you think that is?

## 6.3 Who are your favorite authors?

### 5 Reading

**A** Roald Dahl (1916–1990) was a British writer. His short story *The way up to heaven* was published in 1954. Read the first two paragraphs of the excerpt. What is unusual about Mrs. Foster?

**B** Read the rest. Underline a sentence that shows …

1 Mrs. Foster was probably a traditional wife.
2 the Fosters were most likely wealthy.

### The Way Up To Heaven
**By Roald Dahl**

All her life, Mrs Foster had had an almost pathological fear of missing a train, a plane, a boat, or even a theatre curtain. In other respects, she was not a particularly nervous woman, but the mere thought of being late on occasions like these would throw her into such a state of nerves that she would begin to twitch.

It was really extraordinary how in certain people a simple apprehension about a thing like catching a train can grow into a serious obsession. At least half an hour before it was time to leave the house for the station, Mrs Foster would step out of the elevator all ready to go, with hat and coat and gloves, and then, being quite unable to sit down, she would flutter and fidget about from room to room until her husband, who must have been well aware of her state, finally emerged from his privacy and suggested in a cool dry voice that perhaps they had better be going now, had they not? Mr Foster may possibly have had a right to be irritated by this foolishness of his wife's, but he could have had no excuse for increasing her misery by keeping her waiting unnecessarily.

Mind you, it is by no means certain that this is what he did, yet whenever they were to go somewhere, his timing was so accurate – just a minute or two late, you understand – and his manner so bland that it was hard to believe he wasn't purposely inflicting a nasty private little torture of his own on the unhappy lady. And one thing he must have known – that she would never dare to call out and tell him to hurry. He had disciplined her too well for that. He must also have known that if he was prepared to wait even beyond the last moment of safety, he could drive her nearly into hysterics. On one or two special occasions in the later years of their married life, it seemed almost as though he had wanted to miss the train simply in order to intensify the poor woman's suffering.

Assuming (though one cannot be sure) that the husband was guilty, what made his attitude doubly unreasonable was the fact that, with the exception of this one small irrepressible foible, Mrs Foster was and always had been a good and loving wife. For over thirty years, she had served him loyally and well. There was no doubt about this. Even she, a very modest woman, was aware of it, and although she had for years refused to let herself believe that Mr Foster would ever consciously torment her, there had been times recently when she had caught herself beginning to wonder.

Mr Eugene Foster, who was nearly seventy years old, lived with his wife in a large six-storey house in New York City, on East Sixty-second Street, and they had four servants. It was a gloomy place, and few people came to visit them. But on this particular morning in January, the house had come alive and there was a great deal of bustling about. One maid was distributing bundles of dust sheets to every room, while another was draping them over the furniture. The butler was bringing down suitcases and putting them in the hall. The cook kept popping up from the kitchen to have a word with the butler, and Mrs Foster herself, in an old-fashioned fur coat and with a black hat on the top of her head, was flying from room to room and pretending to supervise these operations. Actually, she was thinking of nothing at all except that she was going to miss her plane if her husband didn't come out of his study soon and get ready.

'Walker, what time is it?' 'Twenty-two minutes past, Madam.'

As he spoke, a door opened and Mr Foster came into the hall.

'Well,' he said, 'I suppose perhaps we'd better get going fairly soon if you want to catch that plane.'

'Yes, dear – yes! Everything's ready. The car's waiting.' 'That's good,' he said.

♪ And baby, you're all that I want, When you're lyin' here in my arms. I'm findin' it hard to believe, We're in heaven

## 6.3

With his head over to one side, he was watching her closely. He had a peculiar way of cocking the head and then moving it in a series of small, rapid jerks. Because of this and because he was clasping his hands up high in front of him, near the chest, he was somehow like a squirrel standing there – a quick clever old squirrel from the Park.

'Here's Walker with your coat, dear. Put it on.'

'I'll be with you in a moment,' he said. 'I'm just going to wash my hands.' She waited for him, and the tall butler stood beside her, holding the coat and the hat. 'Walker, will I miss it?' 'No, Madam,' the butler said. 'I think you'll make it all right.'

Then Mr Foster appeared again, and the butler helped him on with his coat. Mrs Foster hurried outside and got into the hired Cadillac. Her husband came after her, but he walked down the steps of the house slowly, pausing halfway to observe the sky and to sniff the cold morning air.

'It looks a bit foggy,' he said as he sat down beside her in the car. 'And it's always worse out there at the airport. I shouldn't be surprised if the flight's cancelled already.'

'Don't say that, dear – please.' They didn't speak again until the car had crossed over the river to Long Island.

**C** ▶ 6.8 Listen to and re-read the excerpt. T (true) or F (false)?

1 In many areas of her life, Mrs. Foster wasn't a calm person.
2 Mr. Foster may have enjoyed seeing Mrs. Foster suffer.
3 Mrs. Foster was sure Mr. Foster could be deliberately cruel.
4 The writer feels Mr. Foster is controlling and potentially mean.

**D Make it personal** In groups, discuss 1–3.

1 Why were(n't) the Fosters probably a happy couple?
2 How typical are the Fosters of couples who have been married for decades? Are things the same / different today?
3 🌐 Guess how the story will end. Then search on "The Way Up To Heaven" and find a plot summary. How surprised are you by the ending?

## 6 Vocabulary: Evocative language

**A** Read *Evocative language*. Then complete the sentences (1–6) with a form of the highlighted words in the excerpt. There's one extra.

> **Evocative language**
>
> Meaning can often be guessed from context. Writers often use vivid verbs to create an image, whose rough meaning you can guess if you try to visualize the situation:
> Her husband *sniffed* the cold morning air. (= smelled)

1 Her eye _____ when she was anxious.
2 Her eyelashes _____ when he looked at her.
3 My dog _____ his head to one side whenever I open the door.
4 She _____ her hands behind her back.
5 In the market, tons of workers were _____ .
6 My children are always _____ and can't sit still.

**B Make it personal** How nervous do you get when you think you might be late to class or for an important appointment? Do you know anyone with nervous habits like Mrs. Foster? Use words from A.

> I look at my watch constantly, and my eye sometimes starts twitching ...

## 6.4 What do you think of graffiti art?

### 7 Language in use

**A** ▶6.9 Look at the photos. Do you know which countries the artists are from? Listen to two friends, Donna and Jason, to check.

**B** ▶6.9 Match the extracts with the photos Donna and Jason were talking about at the time. Listen again to check.

| 1 | It does look original, doesn't it? I wish I could buy one! | 3 | I have seen some women graffiti artists. | 5 | But his name does sound Mexican. Let me look it up. |
|---|---|---|---|---|---|
| 2 | I did like it. It's just that I really like graffiti with a message. | 4 | I had realized. But still, I always thought graffiti was mainly done on buildings. | 6 | The mural does seem very South American, doesn't it? |

**C** ▶6.10 and 6.11 Listen and read about falling intonation on question tags. Then listen to 1–4 and mark the intonation ↗ or ↘.

> Sometimes tag questions are not true questions, but are opinions. In that case the intonation falls, rather than rises. Compare:
> 
> ↗ The mural seems South American, doesn't it?    ↘ It looks original, doesn't it?

1 You can't call that art, can you?
2 You liked this painting, didn't you?
3 She really has talent, doesn't she?
4 He's really awful, isn't he?

**D Make it personal** In pairs, which is your favorite piece of graffiti in A? Your least favorite? Use some of these words and tag questions to give opinions. Then take a class vote.

> The Os Gêmeos piece is amazing.
>
> Yes, it's so original, isn't it? I can't take my eyes off it!

amazing  bizarre  colorful  creative  dull  (un)imaginative
(un)inspiring  (un)original  thought-provoking  vibrant

♪ Near, far, wherever you are. I believe that the heart does go on

6.4

## 8 Grammar: Using auxiliaries as rejoinders

**A** ▶ 6.12 Read and listen to the sentences in the grammar box and circle the word with the main stress. Then check (✔) he correct rules (1–4).

| Using auxiliaries to express emotions and emphasis | | |
|---|---|---|
| I | **am** | open to appreciating graffiti. |
| It | **does seem** | kind of dull, doesn't it? |
| I really | **did like** | the play, even though the acting was bad. |
| I | **have been** | listening to you! |
| I | **haven't been** | looking at my phone! |
| I | **do not have** | other priorities! |

1 To express emphasis or emotion, stress the ☐ auxiliary ☐ main verb and, in affirmative sentences, ☐ contract ☐ don't contract the auxiliary.
2 Add a form of ☐ do ☐ have before an affirmative verb in the simple present.
3 When a negative sentence isn't contracted, the stress is on ☐ the auxiliary ☐ not.
4 Tag questions ☐ can ☐ can't be used in sentences where an auxiliary expresses emotion or emphasis.

» Grammar expansion p.148

**B** Look at **AS** 6.9 on p.163. Circle six examples of auxiliaries for emotion or emphasis. Then underline the six sentences that the examples are in response to.

**C** Complete the conversations (1–4) about the artists from **7A** with appropriate auxiliaries and verbs to express emotion or emphasis. How many opinions matched yours?

1 A: You didn't like the yellow head in the Os Gêmeos piece, did you?
   B: I _____ it! It's actually cute.

2 A: You haven't looked at the El Bocho piece yet.
   B: I _____ it! I just didn't like it. In fact, it leaves me cold!

3 A: You don't see what's so unusual about Inti.
   B: I _____ what's unusual! Just look at the expression. She represents all of us.

4 A: Maya Hayuk, Kashnick, and Olek all use vibrant colors.
   B: Olek _____ vibrant colors. That's just typical crochet yarn!

**D** Complete the conversations again in a different way, this time avoiding auxiliaries for emphasis.

> You didn't like the yellow head in the Os gêmeos piece, did you?

> I never said I didn't like it! It's actually cute.

**E Make it personal** In groups, discuss 1–3.
1 Does graffiti always need to have a message? Which in **7A** have one?
2 How effective is graffiti in influencing people's ideas?
3 Should the government encourage graffiti as a means of expression?

> Graffiti should have a message. The Olek bicycle is colorful, but it doesn't say anything.

> It does say something. To me the message is that even everyday objects have beauty.

67

## 6.5 Are musicals popular where you live?

### 9 Listening

**A** Look at the photos. In pairs, discuss 1–2.

1 Do you ever go to musicals? What do(n't) you like about them?
2 Are you familiar with any of these musicals? Which others do you know?

**B** ▶ 6.13 Listen to the first part of a conversation between two friends, Stan and Kenna. T (true), F (false), or NI (no information)? Correct the false statements.

1 The name of the book is *The secret life of the American musical: How Broadway shows its guilt.*
2 The book is written for the general public.
3 One of the musicals talked about is *Mamma Mia*.
4 The book compares different musicals, which can be boring for more knowledgeable readers.
5 Millennials may not know that much about musicals.

**C** ▶ 6.14 Listen to the second part. Check (✔) the best description (1–3) for the first part of the book.

1 ☐ From *Oklahoma* to *Hamilton*: a complete chronology of the American musical
2 ☐ A common core and then "an eleven o'clock number": how the typical musical is structured
3 ☐ An experience for all, even those with limited English

**D** ▶ 6.15 Listen to the third part. Does Stan imply the book fully covers the musical of the future? Is it important for the book to cover this topic?

### 10 Keep talking

**A** ▶ 6.16 **How to say it** Complete the chart. Listen to check.

| Recommending books | |
|---|---|
| **What they said** | **What they meant** |
| 1 (This book is) a really good _____. | I really liked it. |
| 2 It's written with a _____ audience in mind. | It's written for all audiences. |
| 3 This book will _____ you _____ on lots of interesting facts. | This book will explain lots of interesting facts. |
| 4 So what else does this book _____ _____? | So what else does this book cover? |
| 5 What's really _____ about the book is that it (captures what musicals have in common). | What's special and noteworthy about this book is that it … |

**B** 🌐 Choose a book you've recently read or research one you'd like to recommend.

1 If it's fiction, note down the setting, characters, and plot, but not the ending!
2 If it's non-fiction, note down the organization, main themes, and at least three details.

**C** In pairs, make your recommendation! Use *How to say it* expressions.

1 Convince your partner to read the book. Make sure your reasons are persuasive.
2 Add in any criticisms you can think of, but make it clear you still feel the book is worthwhile.

♪ In my dreams I have a plan. If I got me a wealthy man, I wouldn't have to work at all

6.5

## 11 Writing: A book review

**A** Read the review about a work of fiction and find the paragraph(s) where ...

1 the character's personality and a conflict are introduced.
2 something unusual about the book is first mentioned.
3 a recommendation is given.
4 the plot and main character are first introduced.

**B** Read *Write it right!* Then match each point to the underlined examples in the review (1–4).

> **Write it right!**
>
> A good book review maintains interest throughout the review. Some common techniques are:
> - praising the author.
> - using descriptive adjectives.
> - contrasting the book with others like it.
> - offering plot details.

**C** Book reviews also contain many other specific expressions that capture the reader's attention. Test your memory. What are the missing words? Then check in the review.

1 As the story _____ , we learn (what a complicated decision that is).
2 We're left with the _____ that she doesn't really wish to leave.
3 I wouldn't want to _____ the pleasure of reading this (absorbing narrative).
4 I couldn't put this book _____ . It was a real page-_____ .
5 I _____ recommend *Brooklyn*.

**D Your turn!** Choose a book you discussed in **10B** and write a book review in about 280 words.

**Before**
Note down the setting, plot, and characters if your book is fiction, and the organization and main themes if it is non-fiction. Then decide your recommendation.

**While**
Organize your book review in five to six paragraphs, following the model. Use *Write it right!* techniques from **B** and expressions from **C**.

**After**
Post your review online and read your classmates' work. Which book would you most like to read?

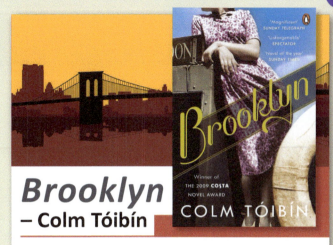

## *Brooklyn* – Colm Tóibín

1 ¹So many books have been written about the immigrant experience in the United States that it would be hard to imagine that anything new could possibly be said. Yet Colm Tóibín's novel *Brooklyn* delivers something very special and unique – a calm, measured depiction of two ways of life, along with the feelings and motivations of the characters that inhabit both.

2 ²The plot centers around Eilis Lacey, a young woman unable to find work in her native Ireland in the early 1950s. Her well-meaning older sister, Rose, arranges a visit for her with a local priest, who's just returned from a trip to New York City. Dazzled by his description of the employment and social opportunities that await her, she decides to emigrate from her home in Enniscorthy, the same Irish town the author is from. As the story unfolds, we learn what a complicated decision that is.

3 Before Eilis's departure, we're left with the impression that she doesn't really wish to leave her hometown and has no reason but the practical for doing so. Nevertheless, she is eager to please her mother and sister. The protagonist, like the members of her family, is somehow unable to express her emotions openly, but ³Tóibín is a master at capturing his character's underlying feelings. Yet perhaps because she is young, or simply passive by nature, Eilis boards the ship as planned, without ever expressing regret, on her way to a new destiny.

4 ⁴The book contains vivid, unforgettable images of Eilis's passage. As readers, we absorb her mood and feelings as she is seasick on the ship and first takes in the sparse Brooklyn boardinghouse where she will live. We are drawn into her loneliness and homesickness as she goes to her job in the upscale department store that has hired her, and then returns alone in the evening. And we follow her avidly as she meets a young Italian-American man and slowly falls in love.

5 Eilis is called back to Ireland as the result of unforeseen family events. I wouldn't want to spoil the pleasure of reading this absorbing narrative by saying more. What I can add is that I couldn't put this book down as I read about her changing perceptions and took in her new maturity. It was a real page-turner, and more than a few surprises await you.

6 I highly recommend *Brooklyn* to anyone looking to understand not only a quintessential American experience, but also the individuality of those who undertook the journey. You won't be disappointed.

69

# Review 3
## Units 5–6

### 1 Listening

**A** ▶ R3.1 Listen to a museum guide discussing the graffiti artists Os Gêmeos. Complete 1–5.

1 Os Gêmeos are known not only in Brazil, but also _____ .
2 Their work includes family, social, and political _____ , and is influenced by Brazilian _____ .
3 Their early influences came from _____ culture, and they started out as _____ .
4 The Brazilian government has commissioned them to paint large _____ and also some _____ .
5 They've become so popular because of their success in appealing to our _____ .

**B Make it personal** In pairs, share opinions about these Os Gêmeos paintings. Use falling intonation tag questions and some words from the box.

> amazing   bizarre   bring out   colorful   creative   dull   (un)imaginative
> (un)inspiring   (un)original   point out   thought-provoking   vibrant

> This one's really bizarre, isn't it!

> Actually, I think it's … . As the guide said, Os Gêmeos …

### 2 Grammar

**A** Read the paragraph. Circle the correct answers.

I'm really sick and tired of ¹[**my neighbors not taking out / that my neighbors don't take out**] their garbage. ²[**With the aim of / In an effort to**] improve the situation, I decided to talk to them. ³[**Given the fact that / Thanks to**] they are elderly, I tried to be understanding. The man wasn't very nice, though, and I really didn't like ⁴[**that he yells / his yelling**] at me. ⁵[**With a view to / In view of**] finding a solution, I explained that I could smell rotting food in my apartment, and that I was very uncomfortable about ⁶[**that they don't take / their not taking**] the situation seriously. ⁷[**With a view to / So as to**] lower the tension, I said I'd give them one more week before I speak to the building management.

Review 3
5–6

**B** **Make it personal** Complete the online blog about two disappointing people, using more formal structures where possible. Then add a sentence with an expression from the box to explain what you've done to improve the situation. Share your information with a partner.

| Given   In view of   So as to   With a view to   In an effort to   Thanks to   With the aim of |

1 I can't accept _____ . _____ , I _____ .

2 _____ isn't very supportive of _____ , I _____ .

> OK, listen to what I wrote: "I can't accept my manager's making me work overtime. Given that I have so little free time, I've decided to find a new job."

> That does seem like a good solution!

## 3 Writing

Write a paragraph about something that hasn't gone well or that you feel you haven't been successful at.

1 Start with an expression in the box and use possessive adjectives + -ing forms.

| I haven't been happy about …   I haven't been comfortable with … |
| I really haven't enjoyed …     I'm very tired of … |

2 Use formal conjunctions and prepositions from 2B to suggest a solution.

## 4 Self-test

Correct the two mistakes in each sentence. Check your answers in Units 5 and 6. What's your score, 1–20?

1 Because of the terrible weather, our plans fell and as a result, our hike was called.
2 I fell flat on my head, and I came close to have a nervous breakdown!
3 In view of I didn't get a bonus, I started staying home on weekends so to save money.
4 I heard about that Bob and Sue broke up last month, but I still hoped they could work things over.
5 I'm going to put a proposal to improve our classroom and try to spell all the steps clearly.
6 Three of five people say you can get used to subtitles as long as you will be open to them.
7 Even though it rains this weekend, I plan to go camping whether anyone else goes.
8 Jim says he really do like the movie because it comes into so many interesting themes.
9 Unless you haven't noticed, our Internet connection is dead, as long as the power is on elsewhere.
10 A good dubbing brings through the personality of the original actors, even if the voices and lips are off of sync.

## 5 Point of view

Choose a topic. Then support your opinion in 100–150 words, and record your answer. Ask a partner for feedback. How can you be more convincing?

a It's essential to fail in order to succeed. OR
  Failure is a devastating experience and should be avoided at all cost.
b Dubbed movies really spoil the experience of going to a movie theater. OR
  Some movies can be dubbed very successfully and have advantages.
c Graffiti isn't real art even if it's creative. OR
  Graffiti is a serious art form and should be given even more attention.

## Grammar expansion

**Unit 1**

### 1 Subject-verb agreement with possessives  *do after 1.2*

In American English, it is ungrammatical to use a plural possessive adjective or pronoun to refer back to a singular subject. Indefinite pronouns are singular:

| **Everyone** should take | **his or her** | seat. |
|---|---|---|
| **People** should take | **their** | seat**s**. |

In informal conversation, you may hear sentences where a singular subject has the plural possessive *their* or *theirs*, but such sentences should be avoided in formal speech and writing.

**Common mistakes**

Anyone who wants to open ~~their~~ *his or her* own business can.

Someone dropped ~~their~~ *a* wallet.

In other possessive constructions, the verb agrees with the subject of the sentence:

| **One** of my parents' friends | **has** | a great new idea. |
|---|---|---|
| **Each** of our team's members | **is** | sending in a proposal. |

### 2 More on expressing continuity  *do after 1.4*

Use the past continuous to give background information, but use *used to* or *would* for repeated actions, and *used to* or the simple past to express a state:

| I **was going** | to school at the time. |
|---|---|
| I **belonged** | to a gym. |
| I **used to / would** | go there every week. |
| I **used to** | have a personal trainer. |
| Eventually I **decided** | to become a trainer, too. |

Use modal verbs in continuous tenses to express ideas that are or will be in progress:

| Probability | You **must be moving** | soon. I can see you're packing. |
|---|---|---|
| Possibility | We **might be starting** | our own business, but things are a little up in the air. |
| Advice | You **should be looking** | for a job. You're already 25! |

Sometimes the continuous verb is close in meaning to a non-continuous form:

| Possibility | We **might start** | our own business if we find a good location. |
|---|---|---|

But sometimes the meaning is very different:

| Obligation / Necessity | You **must move** | within three months. The landlord needs the apartment. |
|---|---|---|

**How long ... ?, *for*, and *since***

The present perfect and present perfect continuous have the same meaning when used with *How long ...?*, *for*, or *since*:

| How long **have you done** this kind of work? | I've **done** it **for two years**. |
|---|---|
| How long **have you been working** here? | I've **been working** here **since 2015**. |

But use only the present perfect with stative verbs:

| How long **have you had** this car? | I've **had** it **for three years**. |
|---|---|

138

Unit 1

**1A** Correct the two mistakes in each sentence. There may be more than one solution. (You may wish to review the rules on p. 9, too.)

1. One of my friends' classmate have an idea for a new start-up.
2. Everyone need to be cautious with their major decisions.
3. Many people worries about investing his or her money.
4. Two hundred dollars are a lot for someone to pay for their English course.
5. Having business strategies are important for anyone who wants their own start-up.
6. My teacher, as well as all my friends, think one of us have a great idea.
7. Keeping your fears in check are important if you're someone who are planning a lifestyle change.
8. Some of my parents' best advice were in his or her letter.
9. Everyone should take their umbrella because something tell me it's going to rain.
10. One of my sister's friends have told me that two years aren't long enough to learn English.

**1B** In pairs, explain the reasons each sentence is ungrammatical.

> Number 1 is kind of hard. I wasn't sure about "friends'."

> You have many friends so that's correct, but "classmate" needs an "s" because there are many students in the class. And then the verb ...

**2A** Circle the correct options to complete the texts about each first time experience.

1. Speaking of "firsts," I'll never forget the first time I ¹[**acted** / **was acting**] in a play. I ²[**was living** / **would live**] in Spain, so the play ³[**used to be** / **was**] in Spanish. I ⁴[**'d been practicing** / **'d practiced**] my part one last time before we ⁵[**went** / **were going**] on stage, but I ⁶[**was still** / **was still being**] nervous. I ⁷[**would worry** / **worried**] that ⁸[**I might be forgetting** / **I might forget**] my part. However, when we finally ⁹[**performed** / **were performing**] the play, it ¹⁰[**was** / **was being**] a fabulous success.

2. It may not seem like a big deal, but the first time I ¹[**was** / **had been**] on an airplane was so exciting. I only ²[**used to fly** / **flew**] from Washington, D.C. to Chicago, less than two hours away, but in those days, it ³[**wouldn't be** / **wasn't**] so common to fly, and it ⁴[**used to be** / **would be**] much more expensive. When I ⁵[**got** / **was getting**] there, I then ⁶[**was having to** / **had to**] take a bus through the corn fields of Illinois up to Wisconsin, where I ⁷[**was visiting** / **used to visit**] a friend. The fields ⁸[**went** / **were going**] on for miles. But what I remember most of all is that a girl ⁹[**had lost** / **was losing**] her knapsack, and the whole bus ¹⁰[**must spend** / **must have spent**] a half hour looking for it.

**2B** **Make it personal** In pairs, share an experience about yourself beginning with "Speaking of 'firsts' ..." or "It may not seem like a big deal, but ..."

> Speaking of "firsts," I'll ever forget the time I spent the night in a sailboat. The wind was picking up, and it had just started to rain when ...

**Bonus!** Language in song

♪ **Some people** want diamond rings. **Some** just want everything. But **everything** means nothing.

Rewrite the song line changing the bold words in order to *only one of us*, *each of us*, and *most things*. Add any other necessary changes.

139

# Grammar expansion

## Unit 2

### 1 Sentences with complements and conjunctions  (do after 2.2)

| In conversation, repetition can be avoided both when you agree and don't agree. ||
|---|---|
| I actually like small apartments. | I **do**, too. / So **do** I. |
| My mom doesn't throw anything out. | Mine **doesn't** either. / Neither **does** mine. |
| I don't like this neighborhood. | But I **do**. Let's at least give it a chance. |
| I'm not happy in this apartment. | But I **am**. And we just moved in last year. |

| You can also avoid repetition with possessives and with indefinite pronouns. When there is a compound noun, only the second noun is possessive. ||
|---|---|
| Possessives | My house is a lot smaller than my **sister's**. My yard is smaller than **hers** also. |
|  | But my house is bigger than **Jim and Amy's**. And my kitchen is bigger than **theirs**, as well. |
| Indefinite pronouns | We don't have a garden, but my brother has **one**. |
|  | Last year, we planted vegetables, but this year, we don't have **any**. |

| Finally, you can avoid repetition when referring to an entire idea or sentence. ||
|---|---|
| Do you feel like going out to dinner tonight? | I don't think **so**. |
| Would you consider renting one of these apartments? | I guess / suppose **so**. |
| We have got a lot of junk here! | I told you **so**. |
| However, you cannot use *so* to refer to a specific noun. ||
| What was your reaction to *this neighborhood*? | I like **it**. |

**Common mistakes**

Our garden is nicer than my ~~sister garden~~. *sister's*
I really like my new home, and my friends ~~like~~, too. *do*
Do you like the apartment? I think ~~that yes~~. *so*

### 2 More on comparatives with *so* and *such*  (do after 2.4)

| Use *so much* before comparative forms of adjectives, to compare non-count nouns, and to refer to a whole idea. Use *so many* when comparing count nouns. |||||
|---|---|---|---|---|
| Adjectives | It's | **so much** | harder | living in a small apartment. |
|  |  |  | less expensive | here than in New York. |
|  |  |  | more crowded | on the subway than the bus. |
| Non-count nouns | There's |  | more information | than there used to be. |
|  |  |  | less time | than when we were kids. |
| Ideas | We like it here |  | more | than we thought we would. |
|  | We miss home |  | less | than we expected. |
| Count nouns | There are | **so many** | more people | that I can never get a seat. |
|  | We have |  | fewer services | than we once had. |

**Common mistakes**

It's so much ~~more noisy~~ than what we were used to. *noisier*
There are so many ~~less~~ people than there once ~~was~~. *fewer* *were*

140

## Unit 2

**1A** Rewrite the sentences, shortening them to avoid repetition.

1. My whole family has trouble throwing things out, and I have trouble throwing things out.
2. There aren't that many good English coursebooks, but I have a good English coursebook.
3. Many of my friends want to get married, but I don't want to get married.
4. A lot of people I know want to live alone, and I want to live alone.
5. I've looked at a lot of apartments, and I hoped to find an apartment, but I haven't found an apartment. (two changes)
6. My friends say their ideas about the future have changed recently, and my ideas about the future have changed. (two changes)

**1B Make it personal** Change two sentences in A so they're true for you. In pairs, compare opinions.

> My whole family has trouble throwing things out, and so do I!

> I don't! My apartment is so small I hardly fit in it myself.

**1C** Correct the mistakes in these shortened sentences.

1. Maybe you don't like small apartments, but I like.
2. They haven't saved money for unforeseen events, but I've saved.
3. My view is nicer than Ted and Mary's, and my kitchen is bigger than them.
4. My neighborhood is a lot more interesting than Sally and Bill.
5. We don't have a pool in our back yard, but my sister has.
6. My parents asked me if I wanted to move, and I said I thought yes.
7. We can't find a good moving company, but maybe you can recommend one good.
8. Our old apartment had big closets, but this one doesn't have some.
9. My boyfriend asked me if I wanted my independence, but I said I didn't think it.
10. I don't know for sure if we're buying this place. My husband wants, so I guess that yes. (two mistakes)

**2A** Complete the paragraph with comparatives containing *so many* or *so much* and the words in parentheses.

> Most major cities have changed substantially in the last 50 years, and Washington, D.C. is no exception. There are ¹*so many more people* (people) than there used to be, and it's ²_____ (busy) all the time. It's true that the Metro, which opened in 1976, was a welcome addition to the nation's capital, one that makes it ³_____ (easy) to get to work. But the trains are ⁴_____ (crowded) than the old buses used to be. Since I still have to drive to a *Park and Ride* station to get the train, I'm aware that there's ⁵_____ (traffic) everywhere, too. And forget about driving to work! There are ⁶_____ (parking spaces) than there once were. In fact, there are hardly any! Everywhere, especially in neighboring Maryland and Virginia, there are ⁷_____ (buildings) and just ⁸_____ (congestion) everywhere. I have to say I like the "new" Washington, D.C. ⁹_____ than the city I remember from my childhood.

**2B Make it personal** Rewrite the paragraph about a city you know, changing the details as necessary. In pairs, share your stories.

*Most major cities have changed substantially in the last 10 years, and …*

**Bonus! Language in song**

🎵 So many tears I've cried. So much pain inside. But baby it ain't over 'til it's over.

Explain why the first sentence in the song line uses *so many*, but the second line *so much*.

141

# Grammar expansion

## 1 More on subject and object questions  `do after 3.2`

**Clauses with question words can be embedded in both *yes-no* and information questions.**

| Does | **whether I have good pronunciation** | matter? |
| How does | **where I study** | affect my test results? |
| Why is | **how my accent sounds** | important? |
| When does | **what we say** | offend people? |

**Common mistakes**

Does ~~how do I pronounce~~ *how I pronounce* my "r" really make any difference?
Why is what she ~~do~~ *does* your business?

## 2 More on participle clauses  `do after 3.4`

**Both active and passive participle clauses, including perfect participles, can also be negative.**

| Active clause | **Not** living near a university, | Jack wasn't able to go to college. |
| | **Not** having driven in years, | I didn't feel comfortable starting again. |
| | After **not** being able to pay her bills, | Amy had to find a job. |
| Passive clause | **Not** respected by his boss, | Elmer decided to quit. |
| | **Not** having been seen in a while, | Marie suddenly showed up. |

**"Dangling" participles, common in informal conversation where the subject is understood, may sound very natural. However, they are ungrammatical.**

| Conversational, but ungrammatical | Not being outgoing, | it's hard to meet new people. |
| Written | | I find it hard to meet new people. |

For clarity, the closer the participle clause is to the subject, the clearer the sentence. For this reason, participle clauses often go at the beginning, and not the end, of a sentence:
**Having loved** the violin as a child, **I** decided to study music and go to a conservatory.

## Unit 3

**1A** Rephrase the questions without the word *it*.
1. Does it really matter what you study in college?
   *Does what you study in college really matter?*
2. Why should it be important how much you practice in public speaking?
3. When is it relevant whether you cram for a test?
4. How does it make you lose weight what you have for breakfast?
5. Why is it my parents' business what I do on weekends?

**1B** Correct one mistake in each question.
1. Do whether I can become bilingual really important?
2. How does what school do I choose affect my career?
3. Why does whether women has children keep them from finding jobs?
4. Does whether do I feel confident as a public speaker improve my performance?
5. How does what our teacher tell us about grammar help us speak more accurately?
6. Does how much TV we watch in English improves our vocabulary?

**1C Make it personal** Choose three questions from **A** and **B** to ask a partner.

> Does what you study in college really matter?

> I don't think it matters too much. Often you end up working in another area anyway.

---

**2A** Rewrite the paragraph, making the underlined participle clauses negative when the meaning requires it. Leave participle clauses that make sense as is.

> My husband and I are both bilingual in Spanish and English, so naturally we wanted our children to be, too. ¹<u>Having been raised bilingual ourselves</u>, we weren't sure where to begin. So ²<u>knowing how to go about it</u> and ³<u>having been given useful advice by anyone</u>, we looked for books in the library. We decided we would both speak both languages. ⁴<u>After giving that a try</u>, though, we didn't think it was working. ⁵<u>Knowing which language to speak</u>, my children were confused, so we decided I would always speak English, and my husband Spanish. ⁶<u>Having tried that now for several weeks</u>, we're all a lot happier.

**2B** Correct the dangling participles, changing any necessary words so each sentence has a clear subject.
1. Not being confident about my accent, it could seem to people that I'm shy.
   *Not being confident about my accent, I could seem shy to people.*
2. Not having been elected president, Tom's attitude wasn't very good.
3. After not graduating last year, it was hard for me to find a job.
4. Not enjoying practicing at all, my violin just sat in a closet.
5. Not feeling loved by his girlfriend, Greg's weekends were kind of depressing.

**2C Make it personal** Share something you didn't do or that didn't happen, and the result, with a partner. Begin with a negative participle clause.

> Not having started my assignment until a day before it was due, I missed the deadline.

> So what happened?

---

> **Bonus! Language in song**
>
> ♪ And promise you kid that I'll give so much more than I get. I just haven't met you yet.
>
> Rewrite the song line beginning with the participle clause, *Having not even met you yet …* Make any other changes needed.

# Unit 4 — Grammar expansion

## 1 More on emphatic inversion (do after 4.2)

When there is a subject and a verb in both clauses, adverbs and adverbial expressions sometimes invert them in the first clause and sometimes in the second. There is no rule. The expressions must be memorized.

| First clause | **No sooner** had I walked in the door | than the police rang the bell. |
|---|---|---|
| Second clause | **Not until** I saw the strange objects | **did I believe** the news. |

Other **first clause** adverbials are: *hardly (ever), never, seldom, rarely, only then, not only, scarcely, only later, nowhere, little, only in this way, in no way, on no account*

Other **second clause** adverbials are: *not since, only after, only when, only by + -ing*

**Emphatic inversion and register**

Emphatic inversion is used in conversation for dramatic effect:
**Never** in my life **had I met** anyone like him!

However, it is especially common in writing:
**On no account can we claim** that these events are real. (written, formal)
**There's no way we can claim** (that) these events are real. (conversational, neutral / informal)

### Common mistake

Not since I was in ~~college,~~ have I had so little money. *(college have)*

Do not put a comma between the clauses when you use emphatic inversion.

## 2 More on formal relative clauses (do after 4.4)

Formal relative clauses often begin with prepositions. When the sentences are rephrased informally, the preposition goes at the end.

| Formal | Jane met someone **with whom** she had a lot in common. |
|---|---|
| | It's an interesting dilemma **to which** I imagine there are no answers. |
| | That's the researcher **in whose office** we had the meeting. |
| Informal | Jane met someone (**who**) she had a lot in common **with**. |
| | It's an interesting dilemma (**that**) I imagine there are no answers **to**. |
| | That's the researcher **whose office** we had the meeting **in**. |

However, sometimes formal relative clauses begin with indefinite pronouns or nouns.

| Indefinite pronoun | The researchers, **some of whom** had different ideas, had trouble reaching a consensus. |
|---|---|
| | I looked at a lot of tests, **a few of which** seemed quite valid. |
| Noun | The test identifies **the frequency with which** we experience these emotions. |
| | We had a meeting this morning **the outcome of which** is still unclear. |

These relative clauses have no informal equivalent, and the only way to express the same ideas more informally is to rephrase them:
The researchers had trouble reaching a consensus **since / because** some of them had different ideas.
The test identifies **how frequently** we experience these emotions.

### Common mistakes

We've finished analyzing the study, ~~which results~~ were very surprising. *(the results of which)*
The students, most of ~~them~~ are under 30, are very open to new experiences. *(whom)*

144

**1A** Rephrase the sentences so they're more emphatic, beginning with the words in parentheses.
1  I haven't had a dream like this since I was a child. (not since)
2  I didn't realize the incident was serious until I saw it on TV. (only when)
3  I only came to understand the events later. (only later)
4  I absolutely didn't imagine our proposal would be accepted. (in no way)
5  Everyone started laughing, so we realized that Ron had made an April Fools' joke. (only after)
6  We almost never consider the consequences of our actions. (seldom)

**1B** In pairs, check the inverted subjects and verbs. Write 1 when the adverbial requires inversion in the first clause, and 2 for the second clause.

**1C** Rewrite the paragraph so it's more formal, using the adverbials in parentheses.

> I just couldn't have imagined some of the truly mean April Fools' jokes I've seen ¹(never), but the perpetrators hardly ever suffered any consequences ²(rarely). Take the case of the friendly and genial office colleague at my former job. As soon as his coworkers had arrived at work, he would invite them to come to his cubicle for a piece of gum ³(no sooner ... than). Of course, they never suspected they might be chewing, and maybe even swallowing, something else ⁴(in no way)! But right when they put it in their mouths, we would hear a piercing scream ⁵(only when)! They almost never knew why it tasted so bad ⁶(seldom). You see, the gum was actually Play Doh, a sticky substance used by children for art projects. My colleagues never found out that it began as a wallpaper cleaner in the 1930s ⁷(hardly ever)!

**1D Make it personal** Using at least three adverbials, share a story about a prank or joke you've experienced.

> Nowhere had I heard about the joke that my friend Hilary played on me!

**2A** Correct the sentences so that each one has a formal relative clause with *whom*, *which*, or *whose*.
1  There are many amateur personality tests, some of them aren't very rigorous.
2  That's the convention center in it we stayed for the conference.
3  I studied the five domains into them our personalities can be classified.
4  Reliability is a trait which importance many people underestimate.
5  The scientist I work with him has just published an article.
6  The roommates, I lived with them as a freshman, were easy to get to know.
7  The woman I lived in her apartment just got elected to public office.
8  Which speed the train was traveling when it crashed was very high.

**2B Make it personal** Make three formal statements about your class or classmates. Your partner will say which he or she agrees with.

> Most of the people with whom we're studying English seem very motivated.

> I totally agree. If you get to this level, you have to be!

**Bonus! Language in song**

♪ Never in my wildest dreams, did I think someone could care about me.

Which word or phrase in the song can be replaced by the word *little* without changing the meaning?

# Unit 5 — Grammar expansion

## 1 More on formal conjunctions and prepositions (do after 5.2)

Most conjunctions and prepositions are neutral in register because often the content of the full sentence determines the level of formality. However, some distinctions can be made.

**To express purpose:**

| Formal | **With a view to** / **With the aim of** / **In the interest of** | reducing costs, the post office has eliminated Saturday delivery. |
|---|---|---|
| Neutral | **(In order) to** | reduce costs, the post office has stopped delivering mail on Saturday. |

Other formal ways to express purpose: *so as to*, *in an effort to*

**To express reason:**

| Formal | **In light of** / **On account of** / **Owing to** | increasing life expectancy / the fact that life expectancy is increasing, people need to save more money. |
|---|---|---|
| Neutral | **Because of** / **As a result of** | |

Other formal ways to express reason: *given*, *in view of*, *thanks to*

**To refer to something:**

| Formal | **With regard to** / **Regarding** | our communication of last week, we are still expecting a response. |
|---|---|---|
| Neutral | **As far as** | prices go, they couldn't possibly be higher. |
| | **When it comes to** | prices, they couldn't possibly be higher. |

In formal speech and writing, shorter noun phrases, as opposed to longer clauses, are often used:
In view of exhorbitant prices, we need to take emergency measures. (formal)
Because prices are through the roof, we need to act now! (informal)

> **Common mistake**
> 
> In light of / On account of / Owing to ∧ you didn't pay your rent on time, we're going to have to evict you.  *(insert: the fact (that))*
> 
> You may also say, "In light of / On account of / Owing **to not having paid** your rent on time, you're going to have to move." Remember: If you use a participle clause, it must have a subject!

## 2 More on objects + -ing forms after prepositions and verbs (do after 5.4)

When changing a noun to a possessive form in a more formal sentence, make certain the apostrophe is in the correct position.

| Neutral to formal | They accepted | **our team's** | submitting a project. |
|---|---|---|---|
| | I read about | **the protester's** | disrupting the event. |
| | We're supportive of | **the employees'** | taking a longer vacation. |
| Informal | They accepted | **our team** | submitting a project. |
| | I read about | **the protester** | disrupting the event. |
| | We're supportive of | **the employees** | taking a longer vacation. |

Sense verbs are not followed by possessive forms:
I saw **the man** climbing in the window.
The cat is in our bed! I felt **it** tickling me.

146

**1A** Rephrase the sentences so they're more formal, using the words in parentheses. Make any other changes necessary.

1. Because we need better security, we will be installing alarms throughout the building. (in the interest of)
2. Since you failed the final exam twice, I'm afraid you're going to have to repeat this course. (in light of)
3. In order to attract more customers, we're going to start doing more promotion. (with the aim of)
4. As far as the complaint you made recently about cockroaches, we'll send the exterminator this weekend. (with regard to)
5. Because we've had so many problems, we may have to postpone our vacations. (on account of)
6. As a result of having had very low sales, we can't offer raises this year. (owing to)
7. When it comes to the interpretation of dreams, I have some good books to recommend. (regarding)

**1B Make it personal** Rephrase the sentences so they are *less* formal. Then choose one topic to discuss with a partner. Any major disagreements?

1. Owing to the many world problems that face us, I don't think I'm going to have children.
2. In the interest of getting a good job, I'm going to delete my Facebook page so a potential employer can't see it.
3. Regarding understanding politics, I'm really not the slightest bit interested.
4. In light of the fact that we live a long life, I think it's silly to watch your diet too much.
5. So as to start over from scratch, I'm going to change schools.

> For the last one, you can say, "To start over from scratch, I'm going to change schools." That could be a very good idea.

> I'm not sure I agree. Even if things aren't going well, it's good to give things a chance.

**2A** Complete the sentences with an object and *-ing* form of the verb, adding any words needed. Then rephrase the sentences informally.

1. Jim witnessed _his daughter's getting arrested_. (daughter / get arrested) And now he's very upset with her.
   *Jim witnessed his daughter getting arrested.*
2. All parents have an investment in _____. (child / succeed) That's why they spend so much money.
3. I'm not happy about _____ so often. (husband / travel) He's never around!
4. We're worried about both new _____ so nervous. (managers / become) Maybe we're about to be fired!
5. The other team has an interest in _____ the award. (our school / win) If we win, they won't have as much competition next year.
6. George resented _____ with his old girlfriend. (Phil / go out) He was hoping to get back together with her.
7. Marcy was aware of _____ about her behind her back. (classmates / talk) They would start whispering as soon as they saw her.

**2C Make it personal** Complete the sentences with the *-ing* form of a verb so they are true for you. Then share two with a partner.

1. I don't mind my teacher …
2. I really appreciate my mother …
3. I'm definitely going to insist on my children …
4. I'm interested in our school …
5. I'm uncomfortable with my neighborhood …
6. I'm grateful for my country …

> I'm grateful for my country('s) taking pollution seriously.

> **Bonus! Language in song**
>
> ♪ All is quiet on New Year's Day. A world in white gets underway.
>
> Create a new song line beginning with *In view of, thanks to,* or *given*. Do you like the way it sounds? Why (not)?

147

# Grammar expansion

## 1 More adverb clauses of condition  (do after 6.2)

Adverb clauses of condition also can be expressed more formally.

| | | |
|---|---|---|
| As long as … | **Assuming** (that) the movie has subtitles, | viewers who don't speak the language can still enjoy it. |
| | **Provided** (that) your novel is accepted, | you'll be on your way to beginning a career as a writer. |
| | **On the condition** (that) the concepts are explained, | all students can understand and enjoy art. |
| (Even) if … | **Supposing** (that) 50 percent have a talent for music, | it's still true that the other 50 percent don't. |
| Even though … | **Despite the fact that** many young people don't like to read, | schools should still promote a love of literature. |
| | **Irrespective of the fact that** we have few museums, | our mayor realizes the importance of art. |
| | **Notwithstanding the fact that** books are expensive, | public libraries are free. |

**Common mistakes**

Supposing ~~the fact~~ (that) your class hates to read, they may still like comics.
Despite ∧ that many movie theaters have disappeared, some still remain.
    *the fact*

## 2 More on emphasis  (do after 6.4)

To emphasize a noun, you may begin the sentence with a *what*-clause.

| | |
|---|---|
| **What a** great **book** | it was. |
| **What** bad **English** | that actor spoke. |
| **What** bad **reviews** | the play got. |

And to emphasize an adjective, you may begin with a *how*-clause.

| | |
|---|---|
| **How bad** the information was | that they gave us. |
| **How right** we were | about Jamie's novel. |

Unlike auxiliaries to express emotion or emphasis (see p. 67), *what* and *how* clauses may begin a conversation. Compare:
A: *What a boring movie that was*! I'm sorry we came to see it.
B: Yes, it *did seem* kind of slow, didn't it?

**Common mistakes**

What ~~a great~~ art this museum has.
   *great*
How enjoyable ~~was the play we saw~~!
             *the play we saw was!*

**1A** Complete the paragraph to create formal adverb clauses of condition that mean the same as the words in parentheses. Do not use the same words twice.

¹_____ (even though) increasing numbers of people move from country to country as they seek employment, newspapers and publishers have not kept up with the need to truly internationalize their offerings. ²_____ (as long as) they speak the local language, English speakers living abroad may wish to read books in their original version, but at least one prominent e-reader based in the United States has been known to offer only an English translation for certain titles! ³_____ (as long as) there is a potential e-reader audience for the original text, publishers should be obliged to provide it. ⁴_____ (even if) some people wish to read translations, it is still true that others don't, just as not everyone wishes to see dubbed movies. ⁵_____ (as long as) publishers can break even on production costs, they need to remember that we live in a globalized age. ⁶_____ (even though) they undoubtedly have a large audience for the translation, they would do well to increase their marketing efforts to reach readers who can enjoy their texts in the languages in which they were originally written.

**1B Make it personal** Complete the sentences with true opinions. Use formal adverb clauses of condition. Then try to convince a partner.

1 _____, all students should be promoted to the next grade.
2 _____, movie theaters should remain open.
3 _____, at least 50% of people my age don't enjoy doing crossword puzzles.
4 _____, many people still never go to museums.
5 _____, I could imagine reading a book a week.

**2A** Rewrite the first sentences in 1–6 for emphasis, beginning with the words in parentheses.

1 That was a really great play! (what) I hadn't heard of the actors before.
2 The writer was awful in the way he expressed himself! (how) I'm not reading anything else by him.
3 There were scary actors that came on stage in the second act! (how) I didn't expect that.
4 She did a really bad job! (what) I'm hiring a different photographer next time.
5 You have an active imagination! (what) A movie like that could never happen in real life.
6 The paintings in this exhibit were intriguing! (how) I loved the artist.

**2B** Complete the conversations. Use auxiliaries to express emotion or emphasis.

1 A: What a boring movie that was. It didn't even have a plot.
   B: But *it did have a plot* ! I agree it was a little slow, though.
2 A: How incompetent that actor was in how he delivered his lines. He couldn't even remember them.
   B: But _____ . I read the play and they were correct.
3 A: What bad news I got today from the museum director. I can't even tell you.
   B: But _____ . I'm always here to listen.
4 A: How stimulating our class was today. I love Shakespeare.
   B: Are you sure? I thought you hated him.
   A: But _____ . I just didn't know enough English to understand him.

**2C Make it personal** Using the models in B and C, make three true sentences with *what* or *how* clauses. Then share them with a partner.

> What a boring class we had last week on American literature! I didn't learn anything.

> But you did learn something! You told me yourself you'd never heard of Raymond Carver previously.

**Bonus! Language in song**

♪ Near, far, wherever you are, I believe that the heart does go on.

Identify the auxiliary used for emphasis in this song line. What is being emphasized?

149

# Selected audio scripts

**2.2** page 17 exercise 2A

J = Julia, L = Luke

J: I've always believed that we attract whatever we think about, good or bad.
L: Uh huh.
J: So, when you can visualize your thoughts, you make them more concrete …
L: In other words, you're saying that a vision board really can help you meet your goals?
J: Exactly.
L: The whole idea seems so far-fetched! You can stare at a picture of a new car till you're blue in the face, but it won't just fall into your lap. It's not enough just to put your mind to something. You've got to do your part and go the extra mile – you know, save money for a long time, if necessary.
J: Yes, of course, you've got to work toward your goals, even if they seem unattainable. But our minds help us do that. If you're clear about what you really want and stay focused, it really makes a difference. I've read lots of books about it.
L: Oh, come on! Surely you don't believe any of this stuff is based on actual research? If we got everything we thought about, we'd have no social problems, no poverty … These people only want to sell books and get rich!
J: You're such a skeptic! Speaking of books, though. Remember that book I told you about? …

**3.2** page 28 exercise 1C

H = Hugo, T = Teacher, M = María

H: Anyway, when I came back to Mexico, I was practically bilingual. Well, maybe not bilingual. My French – at least my spoken French – was much better than my English. But I've forgotten lots of words, and I'm not as fluent as I used to be.
T: So your French is a bit rusty …
H: Yeah, that's the word. And I need to catch up on my reading. It's been a while!
M: You're right. Reading for pleasure is the only way to increase your vocabulary.
T: Well, definitely one good way. But do you agree with Hugo? Do you need to live in another country to master the language?
M: Well, I've never set foot in a foreign country. I've learned all the English I know in this school. And I … I think my English is better than before.
T: Yes, it's improved by leaps and bounds! I mean, you need to be really advanced to use the expression "set foot in"!
M: Well, if you say so … I'm not a gifted learner, though. In the beginning I used to struggle a lot. I was always lost in class.
T: Well, it's natural to feel out of your depth sometimes.
M: I guess. Anyway, I've lost count of the number of grammar and vocabulary exercises I've done. Not to mention all the apps I've downloaded …

T: Yes, I know you have! You've put a lot of effort into your work! And it's paid off! If you're willing to go the extra mile, you can make a lot of progress, whether or not you're naturally good at languages …
M: Yes, and I don't think living abroad is automatically going to make you fluent. Take my dad, for example.
H: What about him?
M: He spent six months in the UK when he was in his twenties, but he keeps saying my spoken English is better than his.
T: Hmm … interesting.
H: Did he use to hang out with a lot of Spanish speakers?
M: Yeah. I think most of his friends were from Mexico and Spain …
H: So that might explain it.
M: But, honestly, why do you need to live abroad when you can access the Internet and immerse yourself in a foreign language without leaving your home? And YouTube is fantastic! When I watch videos, I feel as if I'm there.
H: Well, I'm not sure I agree. Even if you're exposed to a lot of English, it's not the same as actually living abroad. When you live in another country, you absorb the culture … You, erm, you become "one of them," and that's really important.

**4.6** page 40 exercises 3A and B

Welcome to "Today in history," where we review spectacular events you may not be aware of.

October 30, 1938, a day that will live in infamy! Orson Welles was only 23 when his theater company decided to create a radio play based on a famous science-fiction novel. The show aired on a Sunday, at 8:00 p.m, and millions of Americans had their radios on as a voice announced: "The Columbia Broadcasting System and its affiliated stations present Orson Welles and the Mercury Theater on the air in *The War of the Worlds* by H.G. Wells."

Orson Welles, no relation to the writer H.G. Wells, introduced the play, which was followed by a weather report and a music number. At one point, someone broke in to report that a certain observatory had detected a sequence of explosions on Mars, which, not surprisingly, took listeners by surprise. Then the music came back on, but it was followed by another interruption. Apparently, a huge meteor had crashed into a farm in New Jersey – except that it wasn't a meteor, but an army of Martians, which the radio announcer described as "large as bears," with "V-shaped salivating mouths" and "eyes that gleamed like serpents." Not only did the creatures look hideous, they were evil, too, annihilating whoever came their way and releasing poisonous gases into the air, which threw listeners nationwide into a frenzy.

As it turns out, the reports – which had chilling sound effects and incredibly convincing performances – were part of the radio play! The whole thing was so realistic that millions of listeners were under the impression that the U.S. was, in fact, under attack. Panic broke out as thousands of people clogged the highways, desperately trying to flee the attack – where they were headed is anyone's guess, of course! Never before had a radio show inadvertently caused so much panic.

News that the show had wreaked havoc in the country eventually reached the studio, and only when Welles realized the seriousness of the situation, did he interrupt the show to explain what was going on. The nation breathed a sigh of relief to learn that it was all fiction, of course, but the general public had a hard time believing that the show was never intended as a hoax. The radio station came in for a lot of criticism for unleashing terror across the country, and Orson Welles reportedly said that *The War of the Worlds* would be the end of his career. But the opposite happened. Welles eventually signed a movie deal which led to *Citizen Kane*, arguably the greatest American film of all time.

**4.13** page 46 exercises 9C

J = Julie, S = Seth

J: You know, it's not just criminal records. I think censorship has its uses. In fact, I think it's essential in a civilized society.
S: You do? How? I think it's just a cover-up.
J: Well, for one thing, there's such a thing as too much information, most of which you have no need for whatsoever. We have no need to see sensitive government documents, for example.
S: I want to know what my government is up to! I'm not in favor of Big Brother!
J: That may be, but would you know what to do with the information you were given? You might get nervous. Overplay its importance. And you might exaggerate threats. Look at the famous radio play *The War of the Worlds* by Orson Welles. Not only were there no Martians, but there was no attack, either.
S: That's not the same as a real invader.
J: Well, maybe not, but let's take another example: parental censorship. I think it's a good thing.
S: What kind of parental censorship?
J: Like software that blocks access to certain sites. Kids don't have the maturity to know what they're looking at.
S: Don't you think it would be better, though, to talk to them? Why so much control? Seldom do kids not respond well when their parents trust them.
J: Hmm … well, maybe. But how about reading? Shouldn't some novels be banned from school? And kids shouldn't be reading them at home, either, until they're 18. Books can be depressing. They might cause nightmares. And at the very least, they can have a negative influence on young people.

**S:** I just don't believe in any of this. Life isn't a bed of roses. Kids will be more resilient if they know what the real world is like! It's just not fair otherwise.

**J:** OK, one more example. What about history? Should textbooks be honest? This could be really scary. If teachers and textbooks were totally honest, kids might end up not trusting anybody. There's a lot of evil in the world, most of which we don't really need to know about.

**S:** I think it's the opposite. If we conceal information, kids will be suspicious as soon as they find out.

### ▶ 6.9 page 67 exercise 8B

**D = Donna, J = Jason**

**D:** Hey, this is cool! An article on street art.
**J:** Street art?
**D:** Yeah, graffiti artists. Look. Bet you can't guess where they're from.
**J:** Well, their names are right there.
**D:** True, but what's in a name? Pick one. Let's see how you do.
**J:** OK. "El Bocho." He sounds Mexican. In the tradition of Diego Rivera. Didn't he do people like that, too?
**D:** You mean, short and squat? Well, I wouldn't say exactly like that! But anyway, El Bocho isn't Mexican. He lives in Berlin. And he's really well known in the Berlin graffiti scene.
**J:** You mean he's German?
**D:** Not exactly. He's from Spain originally. But his name does sound Mexican. Let me look it up. Wow, according to my dictionary, in Argentina and Uruguay, it means a person's head!
**J:** OK, let's keep going. Os Gêmeos. This artist must be Brazilian. I like him.
**D:** How do you know it's a him?
**J:** Well, aren't most graffiti artists men? Personally, I've never seen graffiti done by a woman. Anyway, I wonder what the name means.
**D:** I have seen some women graffiti artists. And, in fact, next I'll ask you to guess which of the remaining artists happen to be women. But to answer your question, the name means "the twins" in Portuguese. Their names are Otávio and Gustavo Pandolfo, and they're from São Paulo. They've both been painting graffiti for almost 20 years.
**J:** Let's see. Maya Hayuk. She's obviously a woman.
**D:** You get a point! What did you think of her art?
**J:** Hmm … I'm not sure.
**D:** Sounds as if you didn't really like it. Didn't the vibrant colors appeal to you?
**J:** I did like it. It's just that I really like graffiti with a message. And I'm having trouble figuring out what hers is.
**D:** Any idea where she's from?
**J:** Hayuk? Is the name native American?
**D:** I honestly have no idea. But she was born in the city of Baltimore and lives and works in Brooklyn, New York.
**J:** I think we've done enough guessing. Just tell me quickly about the others.
**D:** OK, There's Inti, from Valparaíso, Chile. His name comes from the Incan sun god and the Quechua word for "sun."
**J:** Interesting. The mural does seem very South American, doesn't it?
**D:** Yes, he also likes to draw political themes and represent South America around the world. And finally, we have two more women. Firstly, there's Olek, originally from Poland although she now lives in New York. I read she used to be essentially homeless until her art was discovered.
**J:** You're kidding! I love the bicycle.
**D:** It does look original, doesn't it? I wish I could buy one!
**J:** And the last artist?
**D:** Kashink from Paris. And get this? She's been drawing a thin mustache on her upper lip for a few years and "wears" it every day.
**J:** Cool. I guess you could call that a kind of graffiti!
**D:** Yes. I bet you hadn't realized how creative graffiti could be.
**J:** Well, I had realized. But still, I always thought graffiti was mainly done on buildings.

# iDentities

WORKBOOK

# 1 » 1.1 What are your earliest memories of school?

**A** ▶1 Listen to Chris telling his friend Janet about his first day at college. Number pictures a–e in the correct order.

**B** ▶1 Listen again. True (T) or false (F)?
1 Chris went to bed very late the night before his first class.
2 He arrived late for class because he stopped for coffee on the way.
3 The lecturer saw him fall asleep.
4 Chris doesn't think he was as embarrassed as the lecturer.
5 He apologized and asked to talk to her at the end of class.

**C** Circle the correct options.

I used to work in an office. I enjoyed it at first, having my own desk and talking to customers on the phone, but after a few years, the novelty ¹*wore off / rushed off*. It wasn't the most interesting job to be honest, and my career never really ²*pulled off / took off*, so I decided to leave and go back to college. But on my last day, I thought I'd have some fun, and managed to ³*go off / pull off* a trick on one of my coworkers. He was quite lazy, and every day after lunch he used to shut himself in his office and ⁴*doze off / wear off* for a while. He thought nobody knew what he was doing, but we all did, and thought it was quite funny. So on my last day, he went into his office as usual, and I stood outside his office and called him. I knew he would just listen to the message on the answering machine on his desk and only pick up if he wanted to. I heard his phone ⁵*ring / rush off* and then go to the answering machine. I said, "David, this is the area manager, and I'm five minutes away from the office. I'm coming in to do an inspection." Well at that, he jumped up, opened the door and ⁶*wore off / rushed off* towards the exit, shouting, "If anyone comes, say I'm sick!" We all had a good laugh about that.

**D Make it personal** Complete the sentences so they're true for you.
1 My enthusiasm for _____ wore off when _____.
2 I have a vague recollection of _____.
3 I can still see _____ as if it were yesterday.

3

## 1.2 What innovative businesses do you know?

**A** Complete the conversations with the correct form of these verbs. There are two extra.

| allow | be | have | say | seem | taste | try |

1  **A:** Have you heard Jack's latest business idea?
   **B:** No, and I don't want to. Having good ideas _____ one thing, but he never acts on them.
2  **A:** Have you been to the new vegetarian diner on 16th Avenue?
   **B:** Yes! Some of their burgers _____ amazing!
3  **A:** How's the new business going, Sarah?
   **B:** Terrible. I hired a new assistant and everyone _____ complained about him.
4  **A:** Is this price correct?
   **B:** Yes sir, why do you ask?
   **A:** It's just that two hundred dollars _____ like a lot to me.
5  **A:** What are the results of the latest research, Diane?
   **B:** Well, more and more of our customers _____ they'd like us to improve our support service.

**B** ▶2 Circle the correct forms. Listen to check.

**Why do most new businesses FAIL?**

Statistics ¹*vary / varies*, but it is generally believed that almost all new start-ups ²*fail / fails*. Some people say the figure is as high as 90 percent, which ³*seem / seems* high, but it's a reality. Everyone ⁴*have / has* at least one great idea, but building a successful company ⁵*take / takes* a lot of work and courage. Knowing a few basic facts first ⁶*help / helps*. For example, is the market already crowded? Several hours using search engines ⁷*is / are* a good place to start. Many start-ups also ⁸*has / have* hidden costs that often no one ⁹*discover / discovers* until it's too late. In general, people ¹⁰*make / makes* mistakes with start-ups. Make sure it's not you!

**C** Complete the sentences with an appropriate form of the verbs in parentheses.
1 The company, as well as its customers, _____ at all happy with its level of service. (be)
2 Everyone in the meeting _____ the new product will be a success. (think)
3 One of the managers _____ the new logo. He said it was too old-fashioned looking. (like)
4 Two years _____ a long time to develop a new product. It usually takes about 12 months. (be)
5 About a third of new businesses _____ successful this year. That's a great result. (be)

**D Make it personal** Complete the sentences so they're true for you.
1 Everyone in my class _____.
2 Both my parents _____.
3 These days, a lot of people _____.

4

# How many ways can you use a brick?   1.3

**A** Read the first paragraph. Is the article going to contain good advice?

## The art of procrastination

Do you have what it takes to be a good procrastinator? Or do you worry that you don't spend enough time worrying about not working on that important project? Well, now you don't have to worry, with this helpful guide. Read on to find out how you, too, can join the millions of other successful procrastinators out there, and avoid staying on top of things.

**1** _____

Before you start work, make sure everything is in place. You need the right amount of space, the correct temperature, and enough time. You shouldn't be too hungry or too full, and you need to be able to tune out any unnecessary distractions. Don't even think about starting work until these conditions are met. Otherwise, you won't be able to produce the best work you can do. And only the very best is good enough.

**2** _____

You have to answer every email as soon as it comes in. No one likes being ignored, and people hate it when you don't reply for a long time. Besides that, you might miss out on some fantastic deals and offers from that company you once bought a specific type of coffee from online. How could you, after they went to all the trouble of sending it to you? Only you.

**3** _____

Changing your environment might just let your mind wander. It might even stimulate your brain, and you don't want that winning idea to just hit you like that. You need to zero in on exactly what you're doing!

**4** _____

There's no way you can do any meaningful work if you don't keep abreast of current affairs. This means, obviously, trawling as many news sites as you can, as well as cross-checking facts between sites. You don't want to be ignorant!

**5** _____

And I mean everything. When you're about a third of the way into a task (shame on you for getting so far), stop and ask yourself, "Is this really any good? I'm sure I could do better." If an idea pops into your head about how to do something differently, follow up on it. The best way forward at this point is usually just to tear it up and start from scratch.

Finally, the most important thing: if it's too difficult, just leave it. Never do today what you can put off until tomorrow.

**B** Read the rest. Put the headings back into the article 1–5. Then circle the best advice.

| Keep up with the world.   Don't be rude.   It has to be perfect. |
| Question everything.   Always work in the same place. |

**C** Complete the sentences with one missing word.
                                                                                                              *wander*
1  If you have trouble thinking of ideas, it can be good to just let your mind ^ for a while.
2  It's really hard to work with all that noise going on, I keep tuning.
3  That's when it hit: I could give my presentation as a story.
4  Some people listen to music while they work, but I need silence to really zero on what I'm doing.
5  Sally's best ideas usually pop her head when she's on the bus to work.
6  You need to prioritize these tasks if you're going to stay on of things.

## 1.4 What do the 2000s make you think of?

**A** ▶3 Complete the interview with the correct form of the verbs in parentheses. Listen to check.

PRESENTER: Hello and welcome to *Movie Watch*. Joining me today is movie director Jermaine Gómez. Jermaine, in your opinion, what ¹_____ (be) the most important movies of the decade so far?

JERMAINE: Well for me, one of the best films I ²_____ (see) in the last few years is *Her*, which came out in 2014. Until then, nobody ³_____ (make) a movie that was such an honest portrayal of impossible romance. I mean, yes, directors ⁴_____ (try) to do something similar with movies for years, but it had exactly the right combination of script, music, and acting that made it such a success.

PRESENTER: I agree, it's a great movie. Are there any others?

JERMAINE: Have you seen *Boyhood*? Critics ⁵_____ (describe) it in glowing terms, and they're not wrong. The makers of this movie did something no one ⁶_____ (ever do) before. They filmed it over 12 years, with the same actor as he aged from 6 to 18.

PRESENTER: I ⁷_____ (not watch) it yet, actually, but I'm definitely going to!

JERMAINE: Perhaps the best movie of the decade, though, is *Inception*, in my opinion. With this movie, they ⁸_____ (create) an insanely complicated story, which is thrilling to watch from start to finish, and great fun to try to figure out!

**B** Circle the correct options.

### What ¹*has / had* been the most important technological innovation of the twenty-first century so far?

Many people would argue that it was the iPod. Until it came out, people ²*have / had* bought music on CDs, and some had huge collections that took up vast amounts of space in their home. Others might say the invention of social networking ³*has had / has been having* the most influence on our lives, but it ⁴*hasn't helped / didn't help* our privacy, as we now share pretty much everything online with the rest of the world. For me though, one of the biggest milestones was when IBM's computer "Watson" competed on the U.S. quiz show *Jeopardy*, and won against the two all-time champions. It was important because it showed just how far we ⁵*have come / have been coming* in developing artificial intelligence. Until this point, many companies ⁶*had / have* been trying to develop computers capable of independent thought, and since then, this field ⁷*has / had* been developing rapidly. So much so that you can even talk to your cell phone and have it search the Internet for you.

**C** Match 1–5 to a–e to make sentences.

1 Usain Bolt set
2 3D printing is yet to set
3 The latest album by *Robotix* is set
4 The government has recently set
5 Video-sharing websites have set

a ☐ for a March release.
b ☐ the stage for a new generation of entertainers.
c ☐ a new world record for the fastest 100 meters in 2008.
d ☐ the world on fire, but is expected to become more popular in the next few years.
e ☐ new rules for opening a small business.

## Have you ever had a dream come true? 1.5

**A** Read the autobiographical narrative and circle the correct options.

### A chance encounter

Five years ago, something happened to me that would change my life forever. I was working as a cook in a restaurant on the other side of town, and ¹*I'd just finished / I've just finished* a really long shift. It ²*snowed / had been snowing* all day, so the drive home was taking longer than usual. I ³*just stopped / had just stopped* at the intersection when I felt a hard bump – someone ⁴*was driving / had driven* their car into the back of mine. I was furious.

I got out of the car to speak to the driver, and then I ⁵*had seen / saw* her. She ⁶*was / had been* the most beautiful woman I had ever seen. I couldn't help but remain speechless as she apologized profusely. In that single moment, all that anger and fatigue just washed away. She explained that she ⁷*had been looking / has been looking* for her turn, and by the time she saw I had stopped, it was too late. We exchanged information, and then just started chatting. Before we knew it, an hour had passed and we were both getting cold, so we ⁸*went / had gone* our separate ways. But before we did, we arranged to meet again and go for dinner.

Anyway, we got along really well, and two years ago, we ⁹*have gotten / got* married. She's made me so happy, and she tells me she feels the same, all the time. ¹⁰*We've had / We'd had* a beautiful baby girl, and we now have another one on the way. And yes, we're both very careful drivers now!

**B** Replace the words in bold with one of these expressions with *but*.

| all but certain | couldn't help but | nothing but sheer | I did nothing but |

1 I couldn't believe I'd passed the exam. It was **100%** luck! _____
2 I was so tired the next day. **All I did was** sleep. _____
3 Cathy was **so sure** she would never meet the right person. _____
4 I **was accidentally able to** overhear what they were saying. _____

**C** Complete the conversations with one word in each blank.

1 A: Let's _____ it. We need to find out more about the neighborhood before we decide to move there.
   B: That's _____ sure. Let's do some more research.
2 A: How long have Judy and Kevin been together?
   B: You're _____ me? How would I _____?
3 A: Have you thought about giving sailing a try?
   B: I have, but I don't think I'd be very good at it. Maybe I should just try it and see.
   A: That's _____ I'm telling you. Just _____ it a try. You won't know until you do.

**D** Look back at lessons 1.1–1.5 in the Student's Book. Find the connection between the song lines and the content of each lesson.

**E** ▶4 Listen to the five question titles from the unit, and record your answers to them. If possible, compare recordings with a classmate.

# 2 » 2.1  What would you change about your lifestyle?

**A** ▶5 Listen to the first part of a conversation between Charlotte and Gavin. Answer the questions.
1 Is Gavin enjoying his job?
2 How does his boss react to Gavin's work?
3 What has Gavin been thinking about doing?
4 Does he have a Master's degree?

**B** ▶6 Listen to the second part. What opportunity does Gavin have? Does Charlotte think it's a good idea?

**C** ▶6 Listen to the second part again. Complete the sentences from the conversation.
1 I know it sounds a little _____ - _____ .
2 You can't just sit around and wait for something else to _____ into your _____ .
3 They just seem like really _____ _____ right now.
4 You'll go the _____ _____ and work better.
5 You can still _____ _____ your degree.
6 I know if you _____ your _____ to it, you can make things work.

**D** Rearrange the words in italics to complete the motivational memes. Circle the one you like best.

1 *mile / go / extra / the* – you'll be surprised at what you can achieve.
_____

2 *try / expectations / to / people's / never / meet* – but try your best, and you might exceed them.
_____

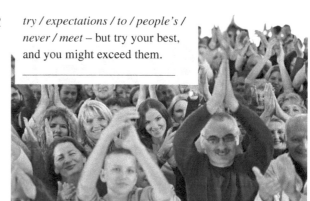

3 *if / mind / you / your / it / to / put*, you can accomplish great things.
_____

4 Go out and find your dreams – *wait / your / into / them / don't / lap / fall / to / for*.
_____

**E** Match 1–4 to a–e to make sentences. There's one extra.
1 I'm sorry, but I'm afraid your qualifications don't meet
2 Alex's explanation of why he was late
3 Chris and Angela are working towards
4 I don't think it's such an unattainable

a ☐ target to increase sales by 20% this year.
b ☐ a solution to the marketing problem right now.
c ☐ the requirements of the job.
d ☐ a lot at stake.
e ☐ was so far-fetched that no one believed him.

8

# What's the biggest house you've ever been to? 2.2

**A** Complete the text with these words. There are two extra.

don't    doesn't    hasn't    have    isn't    to    won't

## MY HOME, MY WAY

*The TV show that follows people as they make big changes to the places where they live*

This week on *My Home, My way*, the Meyer family is having problems. They've just bought an expensive new sofa and realize they shouldn't ¹_____ , as it's going to put them over their budget. They also discover that although they want to extend their kitchen on the side of their house, they may not be able ²_____ . They really like the idea, but it seems their neighbors ³_____ .

Meanwhile, on the other side of town, Joe and Lily can't seem to agree on anything. Lily is eager to create an office in their spare room, but Joe ⁴_____ . He's always wanted to have a game room, but she ⁵_____ .

**B** ▶7 Circle the correct options to complete the excerpts from the TV show. Listen to check.

1 **TV PRESENTER:** So, I hear you've decided on a sofa?
   **MR. MEYER:** Yes, I love this sofa, and Jenny does, *too / to*. We're really happy with it.
   **MRS. MEYER:** Yes, we *have / are*.
   **TV PRESENTER:** But did you realize it's put you over your budget?
   **MRS. MEYER:** Oh no, we *weren't / didn't*!
   **MR. MEYER:** Well, I guess we can dip into our savings, just a few dollars.
   **MRS. MEYER:** I don't like that idea. *They're / It's* all we've got!

2 **MRS. MEYER:** So, do you think the neighbors will complain about the kitchen?
   **MR. MEYER:** Yes, I think they *might / do*. They didn't seem very happy about it earlier.
   **MRS. MEYER:** Oh, but I've always wanted a big kitchen!
   **MR. MEYER:** I know, I *am / have*, too.

3 **JOE:** We need to put stairs in behind this room.
   **LILY:** Oh no, stairs *take / takes* up much too space.

4 **LILY:** So, this is our spare room, which we're going to convert into an office. We've always wanted *to / too*.
   **JOE:** Wait, what? No, we *haven't / didn't*! I thought we were going to have a game room, with a pool table. That's what I told you.
   **LILY:** No, you *weren't / didn't*!

**C** Replace the underlined phrases with one word.

1 I've always wanted a big house, but my husband <u>doesn't want a big house</u>. He thinks it'll take too long to clean!
   _____

2 I bought an apartment last year, but I shouldn't <u>have bought an apartment</u>. I really miss having a back yard.
   _____

3 I love this area, and my girlfriend <u>loves this area</u>, too. But it's just too expensive to buy anything here.
   _____

4 I've never lived away from my parents, and my best friend hasn't <u>lived away from her parents</u>. We can't wait to move in together. _____

5 I've never thought about buying my own place, but I <u>might buy my own place</u> soon. _____

**D** **Make it personal** Rewrite two sentences in C so they're true for you.

1 _____
2 _____

9

## 2.3 Do you like to spend time alone?

**A** Read the people's advice. Match each person to photos A–D.

### How to survive being alone in social situations
Whether it's going to a party or having a meal, how do you survive being alone in social situations? We asked four people for their tips.

**1 Brynn Frazier** ☐ First things first, choose the best time to go. On Saturday evenings, you usually get a lot of couples, so if you go then, you'll most likely wind up feeling lonely. I find the best time to go is in the afternoon. It's less crowded then, so you'll be able to savor your solitude in a space of your own. Also, try to arrive just before the movie starts. That way it'll already be dark, and people won't see you sitting there all alone.

**2 Jerome Wolfe** ☐ I often end up doing this when I'm traveling for work, so I know what it's like. The main thing you'll find is that it can be quite tedious waiting for your dish to be brought out. So take a book, or some headphones to watch a movie on your phone. Reading or watching something while you eat means you'll take your time, too. Don't be tempted to people watch though – other people don't like being stared at while they eat!

**3 Ella McCormick** ☐ People think I'm crazy for going away on my own, or "traveling light," as I say. But I wouldn't have it any other way. I get to go exactly where I want and do exactly what I want, which my friends don't. Even if that means just lounging around by the pool each day! I get to do it guilt-free. I find I experience things much more clearly when I see them through my own eyes, without another person's perception of the experience. So my advice if you're in this situation is just relax and enjoy it!

**4 Alison Taylor** ☐ This can be one of the hardest situations to be alone in, I think, especially if you don't know many people there. If you only know one or two people there, don't be tempted to stick with them all night. Nobody likes a shadow, and you may end up alienating them from other guests. Most of all, don't worry about being shy. In fact, be open about it. Find another guest who is on his or her own and make a joke about it. I did this recently and we got along really well. It also made it easier to mingle with other people as we were together.

**B** Read the advice again and complete 1–5 with the correct name. There's one extra statement.

1 _____ thinks other people might spoil the experience.
2 _____ says you shouldn't take too many things with you.
3 _____ says you need to make the experience interesting.
4 _____ thinks you should be honest about how you're feeling.
5 _____ thinks it's best if people can't see you.

**C** Complete the sentences with these words. There's one extra.

| cater | convey | crave | peace and quiet | restaurants | sense of | tastes | ubiquitous | upscale |

1 Sometimes even very sociable people _____ a bit of _____ .
2 The idea of traveling alone can _____ a _____ freedom to some.
3 When you're in a large group, it can be difficult to _____ to everyone's individual _____ .
4 It's less common to see people dining alone in _____ _____ .

## Are you more of a morning or an evening person? 2.4

**A** Complete the sentences with *so* or *such*.

1 There are _____ many distractions here. I need to go to the library to study.
2 This is _____ a useful app to help organize your time. I recommend you try it.
3 I find it _____ difficult to concentrate in the afternoon. It makes _____ a big difference if I work in the morning.
4 Try prioritizing what you have to do. It'll make things _____ much easier for you.
5 You've worked really hard on this. Thank you _____ much!
6 There are _____ few ways to get a healthy energy boost.

**B** Choose the correct option (a, b or c) to complete the text.

I've recently started doing something new, which has made ¹_____ big difference to how productive I am. Twice a week, I schedule "meetings with myself." I actually schedule the time in my calendar, and during that time, I don't answer emails (I get ²_____ coming in all the time), don't answer the phone, or do anything else. There are ³_____ ways of avoiding the distractions usually, but this makes it ⁴_____ easier. It's made ⁵_____ big difference, and I get through my work ⁶_____ faster now.

| 1 | a so a | b such a | c such | 4 | a so much | b such a | c so many |
| 2 | a so | b so much | c so many | 5 | a so a | b such a | c such |
| 3 | a so many | b such little | c so few | 6 | a so much | b so | c so many |

**C** ▶8 Correct the mistake in each conversation. Listen to check.

1 **A:** What's wrong? You look a bit stressed.
　**B:** Oh, I've just got so much things to do, I don't know where to start.
　**A:** Can I do some of them for you?
　**B:** Thanks, that would help so much!

2 **A:** Kate tells me you've started working from home two days a week.
　**B:** Yes, it's made such big difference. I can work without so many distractions. It gets so busy in our office.

3 **A:** This new organizer app is great. The only thing is, it costs $30.
　**B:** What? Why does it cost so?
　**A:** It's not so expensive when you see what it can do. It's so useful. Let me show you.

4 **A:** How was your vacation?
　**B:** Great, thanks. I feel such better now.
　**A:** Yes, you look a lot better. You were working so much before you went away.

**D** Circle the correct option.

1 Sorry I didn't make much sense on the phone this morning. I'd just woken up and was still feeling *hectic / drowsy*.
2 Can I grab a cup of coffee before we start revising our report? I need a bit of an energy *drag / boost*.
3 I'm so glad the day's over. Time felt like it was really *dragging / hectic*.
4 Things have been really *drowsy / hectic* lately. I've been finding it hard to stay on top of my studies.
5 Kate's really nervous about the presentation. She said she didn't *sleep / drag* a wink last night.

**E Make it personal** Complete the sentences so they're true for you.

1 _____ has made such a big difference to my life.
2 I find learning English so _____ .
3 I have so little _____ .

## 2.5 Can an apartment be too small?

**A** Read Jerry's email to Doug. Does Jerry prefer one of the places or does he like them both?

Doug Owen (dowen@everymail.id)

Hi Doug!

How is everything? Really pleased to hear you're moving here to start college. It'll be great to see you more often. In your email, you ask about the two areas you're thinking about moving to.

Both Lakeside and Oak Grove are nice areas, but ¹_____ . Sandra much prefers Lakeside, but I don't. The lake is great in the summer. We usually hang out there on weekends and grill food outside. ²_____ , it's really peaceful. You won't be disturbed by noise or anything while you're doing your college work at home. ³_____ , for me it feels a bit too isolated. You'd definitely need a car, as there aren't many stores or amenities nearby. Houses are pretty expensive there, too.

Oak Grove, ⁴_____ , is really centrally located. You'd be living a stone's throw away from stores and everything else you might need. Moreover, the public transportation connections around there are so much better than Lakeside. Having said that, it's not as quiet or safe as Lakeside. ⁵_____ it's not particularly dangerous, there is more crime than in other parts of the city.

So what do you think? In my opinion, ⁶_____ good places to live. It just depends what sort of thing you want. Sandra and I are over in Queen's Park, which is near both of them. So you'll have no excuse not to come and visit!

All the best,

Jerry

**B** Complete 1–6 in the email with these phrases.

> although     each has its pros and cons     however     in addition
> on the other hand     the two areas are both

**C** Complete the second sentence so it has the same meaning as the first. Use the words in parentheses.
1. Both apartments have good things and bad things. (CONS)
   Each apartment _____ .
2. The house is huge, and it has a swimming pool. (ADDITION)
   The house is huge. _____ .
3. Our kitchen is modern, but our dining room is old-fashioned. (HAND)
   Our kitchen is modern. _____ , is old-fashioned.
4. Oakdale and New City are cheap places to live. (BOTH)
   The two areas _____ .

**D** Look back at lessons 2.1–2.5 in the Student's Book. Find the connection between the song lines and the content of each lesson.

**E** ▶9 Listen to the five question titles from the unit, and record your answers to them. If possible, compare recordings with a classmate.

# 3 » 3.1   What language would you least like to learn?

**A** ▶10 Listen to three people describing a learning experience. Match each one to photos 1–6.

1   Valeria ☐  Leon ☐  Julia ☐
2   Valeria ☐  Leon ☐  Julia ☐
3   Valeria ☐  Leon ☐  Julia ☐
4   Valeria ☐  Leon ☐  Julia ☐
5   Valeria ☐  Leon ☐  Julia ☐
6   Valeria ☐  Leon ☐  Julia ☐

**B** ▶10 Listen again and answer the questions.

Which person …
1  thinks people have the wrong impression of her? _____
2  gave up for a while and then started again? _____
3  was reluctant to start at first? _____
4  enjoys something which other people think isn't interesting? _____
5  hasn't made steady progress? _____
6  has entered a competition? _____

**C** ▶10 Complete the sentences with one word. Listen again to check, if necessary.

1  I couldn't even get a half-decent sound out of it, and felt really out of my _____ .
2  I put a lot of _____ into it, practicing every day.
3  Although I was a bit _____ at first, soon it all came back to me.
4  Then I started jogging, and, to my surprise, I just sort of _____ it up naturally.
5  Since then I've joined a club, and I've improved by _____ and bounds.
6  People see me as a sort of "techy" person, but I think that's _____ .
7  I always just sort of _____ by when I need to and hope for the best.

**D  Make it personal**  Choose three of the expressions in **C** and write true sentences for you.

1  _____
2  _____
3  _____

13

## » 3.2  Are you into tweeting?

**A** Look at the **bold** words and expressions, but don't read the descriptions yet. Do you know what they mean? Do you use them?

**Trolling**  ¹[is / means / What / to / this] post comments in order to deliberately get a reaction from people. Why it became used on the Internet ²[relates / think / we / to / back] a 17th-century use of the word, which was to use bait when fishing, e.g. use something false to capture the naïve (in this case the fish).

**Meh**  ³[became / this / Why / popular / so] we're not really sure. This three-letter word shows that you're not really interested in something. ⁴[interesting / that / is / What's] it can be an adjective (It was all very "meh") and even a noun (I refer you back to my last "meh").

**Cupertino**  This is the nightmare of autocorrect. ⁵[was / from / came / Where / it] an early spell-checker program which knew the word "Cupertino" (the town where Apple has its head office), but not the word "cooperation." ⁶[was / What / do / would / it] correct the word "cooperation" to "Cupertino" every time someone tried to use it.

**I can't even!**  ⁷[expression / What / know / we / is / about / this] that it began when a social media user finished a comment with "I can't!" to show he or she was speechless with shock or surprise. When the "even" was added, ⁸[really / we / know / don't], but it's clear that it was added to make the phrase even stronger.

**B** Order the words in italics in the texts above to make information-focus clauses.

1 _____  5 _____
2 _____  6 _____
3 _____  7 _____
4 _____  8 _____

**C** Match 1–5 to a–e to make sentences. Decide if each sentence contains a subject clause (S) or an object clause (O).

1 How often people use this expression
2 Whether it's appropriate to send a direct message
3 When exactly we started using hashtags
4 Why social media became so popular
5 What we did to make messages shorter

a ☐ we're not really sure. ____
b ☐ was a result of many different factors. ____
c ☐ was to use lots of abbreviations. ____
d ☐ reflects how much they use social media. ____
e ☐ I think depends on how well you know the person. ____

**D** ▶11 Circle the correct option. Listen to check.

1 **A:** Do you think social media has made us more sociable?
   **B:** To a certain *respects / extent*, yes, as long as we remember to meet people face-to-face sometimes!
2 **A:** I don't get your post. It's confusing to say the *least / mildly*.
   **B:** Meh, don't worry about it. I can't be bothered to explain.
3 **A:** What do you use social media for?
   **B:** Mainly for keeping in touch with my family. It's like a virtual get-together, if you *speak / will*.
4 **A:** I love seeing all the new memes that come out after a big news event.
   **B:** Me too. In some *respects / extent*, it's like a more honest representation of modern culture.

**E** **Make it personal** Complete the sentences so they're true for you.

1 Why people use social media so much I _____ .
2 When exactly I started using social media was _____ .

# Can someone learn to be a good speaker? 3.3

**A** Read and match the types of presenters below to 1–5.

The Animator    The Entertainer    The Lecturer    The Motivator    The Storyteller

## The five most common types of speakers

**1** _____

These types of presenters see themselves as coaches, someone who will motivate you to achieve your goals (often goals that you didn't realize you needed to have). They give lots of encouragement through buzzwords such as "You've got this" and "I believe in you," and you're likely to leave the presentation feeling like you can climb Mount Everest. Be careful though. It's easy to get caught up in all the hype and set yourself impossible goals. And this presenter will make you keep your word. He or she will want to see real outcomes, and if you make any promises, you won't be able to take back your words.

**2** _____

This person loves the sound of his or her own voice, and will use every trick in the book to grab your attention, from jokes to film clips. He or she may have a great reputation as a speaker, spread by word of mouth. Sitting in this presentation will no doubt be a lot of fun, but you may come away wondering if you've actually learned anything useful.

**3** _____

Naturally gifted, this presenter is a real joy to watch. From the get-go he or she will have you transfixed, using compelling personal anecdotes and imagery to guide you through the content of the presentation. It's as if the presenter were born to spread the word. Time will fly through this presentation and you won't want to leave at the end.

**4** _____

This person is lost without slides. He or she will prepare for hours beforehand, gathering data and putting together slides which zoom in and out, with all the whistles and bells. It's entertaining up to a point, but often it'll get to be too much, and you might get motion sickness. If anything goes wrong with the technology, the presenter will come unstuck, tripping over words and generally crashing and burning.

**5** _____

This presenter also loves the sound of his or her own voice, and not only that, often has an inflated sense of self-worth. The presenter loves to back up points with references to books and quotations to show that he or she knows much more than you. Your job is to listen, no matter how boring the style of delivery is. The presenter has to have the final word, so is unlikely to offer the opportunity to ask questions. If he or she does, you won't be able to get a word in edgewise during the answer.

**B** Re-read. True (T), false (F), or not enough information (NI)? Which type of speaker would you most like to be?

1 The Animator is good at coping with problems.
2 The Entertainer is usually a failed actor.
3 The Lecturer has read a lot of books.
4 The Motivator might make you do something you don't want to do.
5 The Storyteller is talented at keeping your attention.

**C** Match the highlighted expressions with *word* in the text to the meanings below.

1 tell as many people as possible _____
2 don't break a promise _____
3 through personal recommendations _____
4 change what you said before _____
5 say the last thing _____
6 have trouble saying _____
7 impossible to interrupt _____

## 3.4 What's the ideal age to learn a language?

**A** ▶12 Complete 1–6 with participle clauses, using the verbs in the box. There are two extra. Listen to check.

arrive   encourage   feel   grow up   learn   meet   start   think

### The life of a polyglot

¹_____ in a family which traveled a lot, as a child Annika Simms came into contact with a wide range of different languages. ²_____ with English, she then went on to learn French, German, Russian, and Turkish. She now speaks more than 15 languages. ³_____ by her parents when she was a child, she would often make friends and "tune in" to the language they used. "⁴_____ in a new country," says Annika, "my parents would first teach me a few phrases. When ⁵_____ other kids, I would try these out, and then gradually pick up more and more of the language. It became easier and easier everywhere we went." ⁶_____ confident in her language abilities, Annika now works as an interpreter for the UN.

**B** Complete the second sentence so that it means the same as the first. Use a participle clause.

1 Before he became famous, Brad Pitt delivered refrigerators.
_____, Brad Pitt delivered refrigerators.
2 Jon Bon Jovi grew up in Pennsylvania and sold newspapers as a teenager.
_____, John Bon Jovi sold newspapers as a teenager.
3 As he was working as a support act, Jim Carrey made a lot of useful contacts in his early career.
_____, Jim Carrey made a lot of useful contacts in his early career.
4 Because he hoped to become a soccer player, Rod Stewart tried out for Brentford F.C in 1960.
_____, Rod Stewart tried out for Brentford F.C in 1960.
5 When she signed her first modeling contract, Cindy Crawford had had few jobs beforehand.
_____, Cindy Crawford had had few jobs beforehand.

**C** Correct one mistake in each comment 1–5. Check (✓) the tips you would find useful.

> **JANA PABLO:** What do you do to learn English? Any tips?
>
> 1 **FRANCISO GUERRA:** Having learn new vocabulary, I write it on little notes and stick them around my apartment, so I see them every day and remember the words.
> 2 **LEE WU:** Where sitting on the bus, I listen to podcasts in English.
> 3 **GABRIELLA VEGA:** After had read a text, I highlight all the new words and look them up.
> 4 **ANNA MACIAS:** Having hearing some new phrases, I try to use them the same day when speaking to people.
> 5 **BRUNO KAYA:** I take photos of signs I see in the city. After having taking them, I go home and look up any new words.

**D Make it personal** Add your own comment with a tip for C.

_____

# What can't you learn through practice? 3.5

**A** Read the essay and choose the best title (a, b, or c).

a The best way to learn a new language.
b It's easy to learn another language.
c How I learned to stop worrying and speak another language.

> I've heard a lot of different advice for learning a language, from studying grammar to practicing speaking with friends. But one thing remains constant: you need to be confident enough to give it a try. But what happens if you're not very confident in another language?
>
> 1 ☐ I love languages, and I find studying them very interesting, but being a bit shy, even in my own language, I've found it difficult. Having made a lot of progress with this recently, however, I'd like to share two techniques that have really helped me.
>
> 2 ☐ First, think of a situation that you always tend to avoid because you worry about how you will cope (e.g. on the telephone). Having chosen a situation, use whatever techniques you can to make yourself understood. And don't be afraid to ask people to repeat what they said, or speak more slowly. You'll often find that the second time you hear something, it sinks in. Over time, you'll start to become less afraid of these situations and your vocabulary – and confidence – will grow.
>
> 3 ☐ A good way to do this is to imagine the worst thing that can happen when you do. People are generally nice and accommodating, and won't laugh at you. If they do, then they're not the kind of people you want to talk to anyway. In no time at all, you'll feel more comfortable making mistakes, and you'll become more fluent – and confident.
>
> These are a couple of ways that have helped me. Nowadays I feel much more confident when speaking another language, and it shows!

**B** Complete the essay with topic sentences a–d. There's one extra.

a Put yourself in a situation where you have to speak the language.
b This has always been my problem.
c Try to avoid making mistakes.
d Remember that it's OK to make mistakes.

**C** Complete the extracts from another essay with these words.

| beginning   first   matter   time   then   while |

> In the ¹_____ , I found making friends really difficult in another language. But after a ²_____ , my confidence grew and I was able to speak to people more. In no ³_____ at all, I was talking to people all the time. Even people waiting at the bus stop!

> Having grown up in the same city all my life, I've never had much contact with people from other countries. ⁴_____ one day I decided to travel abroad for a short vacation. ⁵_____ , I found it really difficult and was very homesick, but in a ⁶_____ of weeks, I was enjoying it. I made lots of new friends and, over time, I came to love traveling. Having been to more than ten different countries now, I'm forever planning my next trip.

**D** Look back at lessons 3.1–3.5 in the Student's Book. Find the connection between the song lines and the content of each lesson.

**E** ▶13 Listen to the five question titles from the unit, and record your answers to them. If possible, compare recordings with a classmate.

17

# 4 » 4.1 How often do you remember your dreams?

**A** ▶14 Listen to Jaylan and Sue discussing an article about dreams. Check (✓) the things it says can influence your dreams.
1. ☐ what you eat before going to bed
2. ☐ good and bad smells
3. ☐ stress
4. ☐ your star sign
5. ☐ playing video games
6. ☐ being a creative person

**B** ▶14 Listen again and complete Jaylan's notes.

* German study: ¹_____ volunteers in two groups
* R.E.M. = the stage of your sleep when you ²_____
* Lucid dreaming = the ability to take ³_____ of your dreams
  Lucid dreamers can ⁴_____ off nightmares
* Creative people are more likely to ⁵_____ their dreams
  Creative people = people who ⁶_____ a lot or are imaginative, according to study

**C** Correct the one wrong word in each extract from the listening.

1. I always take these things with a gram of salt.

2. I mean, there's no worry in my mind that strong smells have an effect on how I feel.

3. With a shadow of a doubt. Sorry!

4. I wouldn't go so long as to say that, but, you know, if you think it's a good idea …

5. The judge is still out on this, but some scientists have made the claim that …

**D** Match 1–6 to a–f to make sentences.

1. People who are very image-
2. Most of the studies into sleep are carried out by consumer-
3. Some dreams are purely stress-
4. The study wasn't very news
5. This new sleep tracker is very user-
6. I dreamed about a ghost-

a. ☐ related.
b. ☐ conscious will often have dreams about their teeth.
c. ☐ friendly. It comes with very clear instructions.
d. ☐ like figure on a beach, talking to me in French.
e. ☐ oriented companies who want to make products designed to help us sleep more easily.
f. ☐ worthy until the results were published.

## Do you believe everything you're told? 4.2

**A** Use the prompts to complete the forum comments.

### What are the worst office pranks you've had played on you?

The funniest thing that's happened to me was just last week. I arrived late for work one day and was trying to sneak into the office quietly. ¹[Little / I / know] _____ , my coworkers had taped an air horn underneath my chair, the type they use at sports matches. As soon as I sat down, it let out this huge blast. Everyone turned around and burst out laughing. ²[Never / again / I / late] _____ for work! *Philippa Evans*

I'm an office manager, and ³[rarely / my staff / play] _____ pranks on me, but on my birthday this year, they all arrived early and filled my office with balloons. I mean they literally filled it with balloons. I could barely open the door! *Lesley Drake*

Last time I went on vacation I told my coworkers that when I got back, I wanted to get a plant for my desk. ⁴[Not since / my previous job / I / work] _____ in an office with no plants. Well, when I got back, somebody said to me "I hope you like your plants" on my way in. I thought it was strange, but only when I got to my desk ⁵[I / understand] _____ . They'd planted seeds inside my keyboard and there were all these little plants growing out between the keys! *Janice Dowley*

**B** Rewrite the sentences using emphatic inversion. Use the words in parentheses.

1 I couldn't find my keyboard anywhere! (NOWHERE)
   _____

2 I only realized I had the wrong bag after I got home. (ONLY AFTER)
   _____

3 We hardly ever play April Fool's Day pranks in my country. (RARELY)
   _____

4 He didn't know that we'd switched his laptop for a pizza box! (LITTLE)
   _____

5 I hadn't felt so embarrassed since I'd been a teenager. (NOT SINCE)
   _____

**C** ▶15 Complete the conversations with the correct form of these verbs. There's one extra. Listen to check.

| breathe | clog | flee | throw | wreak |

1 **A:** This weather's terrible!
   **B:** Tell me about it. It's _____ havoc with my vacation plans!

2 **A:** Have they posted the exam results yet?
   **B:** Yes, and you can _____ a sigh of relief. You passed!

3 **A:** You're late again.
   **B:** I know, sorry, there was an accident that _____ the highways. I was stuck in traffic for an hour.

4 **A:** Terrible what happened downtown yesterday.
   **B:** I know, but at least everyone managed to _____ the fire, so no one was hurt.

**D** **Make it personal** Complete the sentences so they're true for you.

1 Not since I was a child _____ .
2 Rarely do I _____ .
3 Only after I _____ .

19

## 4.3 When did you last hear something illogical?

**A** Read paragraph 1 of Sara's blog. Check (✓) the correct inference about her attitude. What do you think she will say next?

1 ☐ She is suspicious of a post she has read.
2 ☐ She is worried about social media stealing their content.
3 ☐ She respects the person for sharing this information.

### Check it before you share it! by Sara James

"With this status, I declare that all my photos, videos, and other content belongs to me...." Scrolling through my social media page, I see, with a heavy heart, that this status is back again. Worse still, it's been posted by someone I know and respect, as if this is some clever tip-off to show us that the social media site is engaging in a major cover-up to steal ownership of all our data.

The truth is, it's a hoax. You already own all your content. The social media barons aren't some shady burglar, forcing a break-in to your page to steal all the good stuff. Yet hoaxes like this are rife on social media, and I've had enough. So should you. Let's have a crackdown on sharing false information. Here's what I suggest.

When you see a shocking "news" image that portrays something scandalous, and it doesn't sit quite right, do a reverse image search. Several sites allow you to upload an image and search the Internet to find its source. That way you can tell whether it's genuine or just some throwaway post by someone who didn't bother to check it first.

There are also plenty of fact-checking sites out there. These sites trawl the Internet for bogus stories and check their authenticity. Often you'll find that that post about the imminent takeover of a family store by some faceless multinational turns out to be just not true.

You can also just check the sources of the post yourself. If it comes from a site called something like "clicksrus.com" or "welovesunglasses.com," then you can bet your bottom dollar it's not real. Search for the story yourself. If it comes up in established newspaper sites, then it might just be authentic.

Finally, call people out when they post hoaxes as if they were true. It's important we do this if we want to prevent a complete wipeout of the truth online. But be nice about it. That's why it's called "social" media, after all. So instead of saying, "This is nonsense," you could write a comment like, "You may want to run this story by a fact-checking website first."

**B** Choose the correct option (a, b or c).

1 Sara thinks false posts are ...
 a rare. b common. c too long.
2 A reverse image search allows you to find out ...
 a if a photo has been altered.
 b who the people in a photo are.
 c where an image came from.
3 Fact-checking websites _____ false stories on the Internet.
 a look for b share c create
4 Which of these does Sara NOT say you can do yourself?
 a pay to find out if a story is real
 b tell if a story is false by its web address
 c see if a story is credible by looking at other places it appears
5 What does Sara ask us to do at the end of her blog?
 a tell people a story that they posted is nonsense
 b tell people a story is false if they post it
 c search for a story someone posted on a fact-checking website

**C** Find seven nouns / adjectives formed from phrasal verbs in the article. Match them to definitions 1–7.

1 entering a building illegally and by force _____
2 disposable _____
3 destruction _____
4 action that is taken to deal strictly with a problem or a crime _____
5 an attempt to hide the truth _____
6 a secret warning _____
7 assuming control over a company _____

**D** **Make it personal** Complete the sentences so they're true for you.

1 When I'm online I often _____.
2 Most social media users tend to _____.
3 Sometimes I do things which might _____.

# How would you describe your personality? 4.4

**A** Match 1–5 to a–e to make sentences with formal relative clauses.

1. A hundred people were studied,
2. It's important that we remember the work of Professor Richards,
3. It's a well-known personality test,
4. We now have the results of the research,
5. There are hundreds of people

a ☐ for whom this personality trait is desirable.
b ☐ without whom the discovery wouldn't have been possible.
c ☐ from which we can conclude that certain personality types crave attention.
d ☐ about which many books have been written.
e ☐ most of whom had some kind of undesirable personality trait.

**B** Complete the texts with these words and phrases.

| about which | whom | towards which | in which | most of whom | which |

## INVOLUNTARY EXPRESSION DISORDER (IED)

This is an actual condition ¹_____ people have uncontrollable emotional expressions. They might have heard that something terrible has happened to someone, ²_____ they love and care for, but all they can do is laugh uncontrollably. The condition, ³_____ very little is still known, is also called pseudobulbar affect.

## PERSONALITY TRAIT OR MEDICAL DISORDER?

## OPPOSITIONAL DEFIANT DISORDER (ODD)

People with this condition don't respond well to authority, ⁴_____ they can become hostile, angry, or vindictive. This isn't just the normal rejection of authority, ⁵_____ most children experience at one point or another. It goes much further than that. A person with ODD can continuously cause problems for at least six months.

## ALEXITHYMIA

This is a disorder where people are simply unable to express their feelings or emotions. It affects about 10% of the population, ⁶_____ also have trouble reading the expressions of others.

**C** ▶16 Decide if the **bold** letter s is pronounced /s/ (S) or /z/ (Z). Listen to check.

1. **A:** What do you think of the idea in the article?
   **B:** Well, it's an interesting hypothe**s**is, but I'd take it with a grain of salt. ☐ ☐
2. **A:** Oh, you're *such* a kind person.
   **B:** Enough of your **s**arca**s**m! ☐ ☐
3. **A:** Do you ever u**s**e personality tests at your company? ☐
   **B:** Oh, yes, we make u**s**e of them all the time. ☐
4. **A:** What are these figures ba**s**ed on? ☐
   **B:** They're taken from each pha**s**e of the research we've carried out. ☐

21

## 4.5 Would you ever hire a former criminal?

**A** Number the paragraphs of the letter to a newspaper in order (1–6).

**By James Hartfield**

a ☐ First, there is some ¹_____ as to whether conspiracy theories actually keep the government (whom we should certainly question) in check. In fact, once they are inevitably shown to be the nonsense that they are, they give credibility to the government that denied the claims in the first place. The truth always comes out in the end.

b ☐ For all of the reasons above, I urge you to stop publishing such theories, and make sure people who push them are banned from being published in this newspaper again. It's up to us to check the facts, so let's put this nonsense to bed, once and for all.

c ☐ Many letters in this newspaper have perpetuated various ridiculous conspiracy theories of late, one of which is the suggestion that Elvis Presley is still alive and well, and has been spotted working at a gas station in the Midwest. I ²_____ believe that we need to stop peddling this nonsense and rely on the facts at hand.

d ☐ Second, ³_____ of how much individuals believe what they say, conspiracy theories can be disrespectful towards the people involved. For example, despite ridiculous ⁴_____ to the contrary, Man did actually set foot on the moon in 1969. It wasn't a staged production in the desert. No one is trying to conceal information here.

e ☐ Many would ⁵_____ that conspiracy theories provide a useful check on state power, as they force us to question what we are told in the media. While there is no denying that we should cast a critical eye (or ear) on everything we are told, there are compelling reasons not to do so by way of conspiracy theories.

f ☐ Finally, the abundance of conspiracy theories can prevent people from fact-checking stories for themselves, especially when shared on social media. Sharing a post might seem to mean putting the facts on the table. This can only lead to a general dumbing down of the population.

**B** Complete the letter with these words. Do you agree with James?

| argue   claims   debate   irrespective   strongly |

**C** Match the highlighted expressions in the letter to these definitions.
1 eventually we will see the real situation _____
2 out in the open for everyone to see _____
3 our responsibility/choice _____
4 hide the facts _____
5 make it so that someone is not allowed to do something _____

**D** Look back at lessons 4.1–4.5 in the Student's Book. Find the connection between the song lines and the content of each lesson.

**E** ▶17 Listen to the five question titles from the unit, and record your answers to them. If possible, compare recordings with a classmate.

# 5 » 5.1 Why do good plans sometimes fail?

**A** ▶18 Listen to Marta and Liam discussing an article about publicity stunts. True (T) or false (F)?
1 The AApass allowed you to travel as much as you wanted.
2 American Airlines expected people to fly as often as they did.
3 The CEO didn't realize his identity had been stolen until later.
4 The design of the "walkie-talkie" building made the air inside it very hot.

**B** ▶18 Listen again. What does each number refer to?
1 1981 _____
2 250,000 _____
3 50 million _____
4 1994 _____
5 2007 _____
6 13 _____
7 250 million _____
8 91 _____

**C** ▶19 Complete the extracts from the conversation. Listen to check.
1 Well, in the end, they realized it was a major _____ not to have anticipated customer reactions and decided to _____ the whole thing off.
2 It was a high-_____ plan, and one that fell flat on its face, too.
3 So his plans to demonstrate how secure the company was definitely fell _____.
4 When they were on the _____ of completing it, they noticed a _____.

**D** Choose the correct alternative to complete the conversations.
1 A: I'm really proud of what you've achieved since you lost your job.
   B: Thanks. It took me a while to *hold / pull* myself together, but I got there in the end.
2 A: So, how did the publicity event go?
   B: It fell flat on its *face / legs*. The band didn't even show up.
3 A: I can't believe it. After all that work, we're back to square *two / one*.
   B: I know, but at least we get to try out something new now.
4 A: Are you enjoying your job?
   B: Oh, yes, thanks, much better than the last place. I came this close *by / to* having a nervous breakdown there!
5 A: What was all that commotion in town the other day?
   B: Didn't you hear? That big clothing store had a sale and things got out of *hand / hands*. People were fighting each other to get the bargains.

**E Make it personal** Complete the sentences so they're true for you.
1 I was on the verge of _____ when _____.
2 Recently I came this close to _____.

23

## 5.2 Do you ever make resolutions?

**A** Complete the text with these words.

| aim | as | effort | given | thanks | view |

**Going the extra mile**

¹_____ the fact that most of us lead very busy lives, it's important to set ourselves goals intelligently, so ²_____ to ensure success. With the goal or ³_____ of making this easier, companies often tell their employees to set goals which are S.M.A.R.T. (Specific, Measurable, Achievable, Realistic, and Timely). Specific, measurable, and timely are definitely good ideas. But in an ⁴_____ to achieve great things, do we really want to set goals which are easily achievable and realistic? ⁵_____ to easy, achievable goals, we may never realize our true potential. After all, with a ⁶_____ to pushing his employees above and beyond, it was Steve Jobs who said, "We're here to put a dent in the universe."

**B** Match 1–5 to a–f to make sentences. There's one extra.

1 With the aim of making them easier to achieve,
2 In view of his health problems,
3 In an effort to reduce stress among employees,
4 Thanks to lower flight costs,
5 So as to lose weight,

a ☐ many people are traveling further on their vacations.
b ☐ Paul has decided to take some time off from work.
c ☐ big goals are usually broken down into smaller ones.
d ☐ I've decided to join a gym.
e ☐ the company is offering free meditation classes.
f ☐ more companies are charging higher fees.

**C** Circle the correct options.

It's the same every year on January 1st. We decide we're going to make a ¹*fresh / up-to-date* start and set ourselves bold New Year's resolutions. We ²*hold / get* our act together for the first month, but by February, our enthusiasm is already starting to falter. So how can we make sure we succeed and follow ³*through / on* with our plans? The first thing is to create a new habit. Unless it's a habit, you won't succeed. You don't need to completely start ⁴*new / anew*, just introduce small changes which you can keep. For example, instead of sitting down in front of the TV after dinner, why not go for a ten-minute walk? You may even end up going for a longer walk after a while. If you didn't eat very healthily last year, you don't need to completely turn the ⁵*page / book* and stick to salad. Just start by introducing healthier food into your diet. An apple a day is an easy way to do this, and it's full of healthy fiber, too. There's no need to reinvent yourself. Making small changes which become habits will help you stick ⁶*to / on* your plans.

**D Make it personal** Rewrite the sentences so they're true for you.

1 In an effort to save money, I've started walking to work/school.
_____

2 Thanks to playing sports, I keep in shape and stay healthy.
_____

3 With the aim of eating more healthily, I've started eating more fruit.
_____

## How well do you deal with failure? 5.3

**A** Read the introduction to the website. Which of these things does the website NOT ask people to share?
1 an experience
2 reasons why failure is important
3 something positive that came from the experience

### Online Failure Festival

Everyone hates to fail, but is it always a bad thing? We say no! In fact, we believe that failure is important to learn the things we need to know in order to succeed. What's your failure story, and what did you learn from it? Share your story with us below for the chance to win a great prize.

Last year, I entered a marathon and failed miserably. Because I've been running for years (though never as far as a marathon), I didn't think I needed to follow a special training plan or anything. A marathon really is a different beast from shorter distances, and at 20 miles in, I crashed and burned, or "hit the wall" as they say, and couldn't finish. I was devastated, and held on to this failure for a long time. I even stopped running for a while. But it was good for me in the end as it made me take stock, look at how I was training, and start again properly this time. This year, I entered a new marathon and went to great lengths to train properly. I had a great race and finished in under four hours.
*Steve, Montreal*

A few years ago, I had an idea for a new app which I believed could be really successful. I got together with a few of my friends, left my job, and we decided to launch it as part of a new business. To cut a long story short, it didn't do nearly as well as we expected, and, within a year, we had to close the company. Fortunately, I'm now working again at a large software company. The experience actually taught me a lot. Rather than dwell on the failure of the app, I learned a lot of things about launching a new product, which has given me new skills that I can now use on my job.
*Vanda, San Francisco*

I just published my first novel, after years of having it rejected by publishers. It can be really hard to face constant rejection, and there were times when I really thought I would never get it published. But I kept things in perspective. I strongly believe there can be no success without failure. The important thing is to put those failures behind you and learn from them. Now that I'm finally getting it published, it makes all the smaller failures worthwhile.
*Carla, Delaware*

**B** Read the people's comments on the website and complete 1–5 with the correct name. There's one extra comment.
1 _____ says the experience taught him / her things that are useful now.
2 _____ says the experience stopped him / her doing what he / she wanted for some time.
3 _____ says he / she would never make the same mistake again.
4 _____ thinks it's his / her own fault that he / she didn't succeed.
5 _____ thinks determination is important to succeed.

**C** ▶20 Complete the sentences with the correct form of phrases from the website. Listen to check.
1 Steve _____ the fact that he didn't finish the marathon for a long time.
2 Eventually he _____ of the situation and started training again.
3 He _____ to make sure he was properly prepared the second time.
4 Vanda didn't _____ the fact that her business failed.
5 After being rejected, Carla tried to _____ things _____ .
6 She thinks you should _____ failures _____ .

**D Make it personal** Complete the sentences so they're true for you.
1 I've recently gone to great lengths to _____ .
2 I try not to dwell on _____ .

## 5.4 Have you ever had a wrong first impression?

**A** Complete the social media comments with appropriate words.

**Nina Blank:** What's the most disastrous date you've ever been on?

**Jackie Singleton:**
I went to dinner recently with a really boring guy. He kept insisting on ¹_____ listening to him talking about himself.

**Ryan McGuire:**
I met a woman who was really nice, until she started talking about politics. She went on and on about how she was against ²_____ introducing healthcare reforms. She wouldn't let me get a word in edgewise.

**Thomas Murphy:**
I'm sick of ³_____ standing me up on dates. The last time, we went to watch a movie. She left "to get popcorn" and never came back.

**Daniela McDonald:**
It wasn't until after the date that I learned about ⁴_____ need for constant attention. We had a really nice lunch, but then later that afternoon and evening, he called me 10 times!

**Landon Dawson:**
She looked stunning. Fortunately, I'd made an effort and was wearing my new white shirt. I wasn't so impressed by ⁵_____ accidentally spilling orange juice down it!

**B** Correct the mistake in these sentences.
1 I can't stand my girlfriend is talking about her ex all the time. _____
2 I'm not happy about my parents' who complaining about my boyfriend. _____
3 Russ and Ella are so in love. It's so nice to see they always doing things together. _____
4 Where have you been? I was counting on you made me feel better about what happened today. _____
5 I'm sick of he's talking about his friends all the time. _____

**C** Circle the correct options.
1 **A:** Did you find someone to help you with your project in the end?
   **B:** Yes, I teamed up *for / with* a couple of others in my class, and we finished it in no time.
2 **A:** Did you work things *out / up* with your brother?
   **B:** I did. Things went well in the end, and we're friends again.
3 **A:** I was really counting *to / on* Joe to help me with my assignment, but he didn't do anything.
   **B:** Why don't you take the issue *up / on* with your professor? It's not fair that you should do all the work.
4 **A:** I'm really sorry I embarrassed you in front of your parents.
   **B:** It's OK. I'll let you *off / out*.
5 **A:** Phew! I was worried we wouldn't be able to stick *on / to* the deadline there.
   **B:** Me too, but your help was fantastic. I thought we'd wind *up / out* not finishing in time, but we made it. Thanks a million.

# How bad are drivers where you live? 5.5

**A** Read the proposal. Which of these supporting arguments does Shaun Hogan NOT make?

The proposal ...
1 will make the area safer.   2 is cheap.   3 will help educate young people.

| To: | City Hall |
| From: | Shaun Hogan |
| Subject: | Proposal for community service program |

Dear Ms. Wheeler:

As I'm sure you're aware, the trash problem in our local area has become quite a problem recently. Budget cuts to local services mean there simply aren't enough people to deal with it effectively, and it's taking its toll on the cleanliness of our neighborhood.

As president of the Fairtown Residents' Association, I'm writing to suggest a proposal we have discussed at length in our weekly meetings: We would like to team up with local schools to establish a community service cleaning project, involving local teenagers as part of normal school hours. This would involve classes of teenagers going out into the local community once a week for two hours to pick up trash from the streets.

¹Br_____ sp_____ , it would have two goals: (1) to improve the cleanliness of the neighborhood, and (2) to involve young people in the community and teach them the importance of looking after their local area.

²Es_____ , this would provide a solution to the lack of budget funds to clean the local area.
³Cl_____ , the funds available at the moment aren't sufficient. ⁴Ad_____ , it wouldn't completely provide a solution, but when coupled with existing services, it would make a difference. ⁵In_____ , there is also the possibility of the students sorting through saleable recyclable material.

⁶Ob_____ , this would provide benefits to the teenagers involved. We believe that it would be empowering for young people in the local area. It will allow them to feel part of the community, and responsible for how it looks.
⁷Fr_____ , they may even wind up feeling proud of their area. This would be an important step in reducing the amount of trash they drop on the streets, too.

I hope I have managed to provide convincing arguments to why this plan will work. Please feel free to contact me if you have any questions or to discuss how to move forward with the proposal.

Sincerely,

Shaun Hogan

**B** Complete the proposal with the missing adverbial expressions 1–7. The first two letters are provided.

**C** Circle the correct options.

1 **A:** What does your proposal *entail / turn down*?
   **B:** Well, the general idea is that we create a no parking zone on the main avenue.
2 **A:** Is our proposal *rationale / airtight*?
   **B:** Yes, it is. It *spells out / turns down* all the different steps involved in the project.
3 **A:** Have you *put together / re-read* that proposal yet?
   **B:** Yes, I have. And I'm afraid they put *it together / turned it down*.
   **A:** OK, well let's *spell it out / redo it* together and see if we can get it accepted.

**D** Look back at lessons 5.1–5.5 in the Student's Book. Find the connection between the song lines and the content of each lesson.

**E** ▶21 Listen to the five question titles from the unit, and record your answers to them. If possible, compare recordings with a classmate.

# 6 » 6.1 Do you still read paper books?

**A** ▶22 Listen to part of a webinar on how to be a successful content writer. Number the topics a–d in the order they're mentioned.

a ☐ writing original content
b ☐ writing different types of content
c ☐ publicizing your content
d ☐ finding out information to support what you say

**B** ▶22 Listen again and choose the correct option (a, b, or c).

1 Writing good content is important because …
  a nowadays people have a lot of choice about what they decide to read.
  b it's difficult to choose an interesting topic to write about.
  c it's difficult to compete with traditional books and journals.
2 "Listicles" are …
  a articles about a particular group of people.
  b things we write to help us remember to do things.
  c articles with a number in the titles.
3 You can check if information in an article is true by …
  a reading it carefully for any contradictions.
  b crossing out incorrect facts.
  c finding the same information in a number of other sources.
4 If your writing style is original …
  a the way you say things will be less important than what you say.
  b people will know who's written it.
  c it will be popular.
5 A social media presence is important to …
  a demonstrate what you can write to the right people.
  b let people know you are looking for work.
  c look for ideas to include in your own work.

**C** ▶23 Complete the extracts from the webinar with the correct form of these phrasal verbs. Listen to check.

> bring out    cross out    pick out    point out    wear out    work out

1 Being a successful content writer means creating stunning content which people will _____ to read.
2 Today, I'm going to show you how to write content that _____ the best of your work.
3 Successful content writers are able to _____ how to write in the appropriate style for the medium.
4 Opinion pieces, on the other hand, are often persuasive and well-researched, _____ facts that support your argument.
5 You might even want to delete the fact. You can just _____ it _____ and start again.
6 Once you've realized, you'll never _____ your welcome.

**D Make it personal** Write your answers to the questions.

1 Which do you prefer to do: work out the meaning of new words in a text yourself, or look them up? Why?

_____

2 What or who brings out the best in you? In what way?

_____

3 Describe a favorite item of clothing that's worn out but you still wear it.

## Do you ever watch dubbed movies? 6.2

**A** Circle the correct adverbials.

### The future of movies

Developments in technology over the last thirty years have transformed the way we watch movies. But what's in store for the future? ¹*Unless / As long as* you hate watching movies, you'll find some of the developments that are just around the corner very exciting.

First of all, there's immersive audio, or 3D sound. This enables producers to place sounds at specific places around the movie theater, ²*in case / even if* the speakers are in different locations in different theaters. And full immersion doesn't just apply to audio, either. Many studios are working towards true 3D movies, so that you don't look at a screen, but see the action going on all around you. But don't worry. There will still be "traditional" options available ³*whether or not / in case* you think that's too much.

And why stop at 3D? Some movie theaters will be able to offer 4D, ⁴*as long as / unless* they have the right equipment. So, for example, when it starts raining on screen, small jets will spray water at you. Perhaps not everyone's idea of fun! But ⁵*even if / whether or not* you like these changes, they are certain to change the way we watch movies.

**B** Complete the conversations with adverbials from **A**.

1. **A:** I'm not sure about true 3D. Where would you know where to look?
   **B:** Yes, you'd be constantly looking around _____ you missed something. Sounds tiring.
2. **A:** I like the idea of true 3D, _____ it's not a horror movie.
   **B:** Exactly, can you imagine zombies creeping up behind you?!
3. **A:** I love the idea of 4D effects.
   **B:** You do? I wouldn't go to the movies _____ I was wearing waterproof clothing!
4. **A:** I'm not sure I like the idea of these innovations. They don't sound very relaxing.
   **B:** Yes, but _____ you like them, you have to admit they're very interesting.
5. **A:** Do you go to the movies a lot?
   **B:** No, and I'll always prefer watching at home, _____ these innovations happen.

**C** ▶24 Complete the comments about a movie with these words. There's one extra. Listen to check.

| curiosity | money | patience | sheer habit | sync | the theater | 10 |

"
1. It was so boring, I walked out of _____ half way through.
2. I'd never heard of this movie before, so just went to see it out of _____ . I'm glad I did. It was amazing.
3. It's a good movie, but the subtitles and sound were a bit out of _____ , which made it difficult to follow at times.
4. Nine out of _____ of this director's movies are a flop. This was the 1 out of 10, fortunately.
5. It takes a long time for the action to start, and I nearly ran out of _____ . But then it did, and I'm glad I waited.
6. I often choose action movies just out of _____ , so this time I decided to watch a comedy, and really enjoyed it.
"

**D Make it personal** Complete the sentences so they're true for you.

1. I never go to the movies unless _____.
2. I like watching movies at home as long as _____.

## 6.3 Who are your favorite authors?

**A** Read the article. Match topics 1–6 to paragraphs a–e. There's one extra topic.

1. ☐ how he started writing children's books
2. ☐ what the writer finds fascinating about Roald Dahl
3. ☐ his legacy
4. ☐ the idea for a famous children's book
5. ☐ his books that were made into movies
6. ☐ some of Roald Dahl's earlier jobs

### Roald Dahl *A story of a life*

a  I've always loved reading Roald Dahl's stories, not only as a child but also more recently again as an adult. It always amazed me how one man could create such vivid worlds of imagination with such universal appeal. And now, standing here in the Roald Dahl museum, set in a small village about thirty minutes from London, where he lived and wrote the stories, I'm starting to realize how he was able to do so.

b  They say you should write about what you know, even if it doesn't seem that interesting to you. Well, Roald Dahl certainly had a wealth of source material. Before becoming a writer, he worked as an explorer for an oil company, a World War II fighter pilot (fighting in such major battles as the Battle of Athens), a diplomat, and an intelligence officer. In fact, it was during his time as an officer that he wrote his first published work, *A Piece of Cake*, about his wartime adventures.

c  His first children's book (the genre he is most famous for) was called *The Gremlins*, and was about badly-behaved mythical creatures who bustled about, making the lives of World War II fighter pilots difficult in any way they could. But most of his inspiration for his children's stories came from his own childhood. When he was eight, he and four of his friends were punished for putting a dead mouse in a jar of gobstoppers (a popular candy in the UK with children in the 1920s) in the local candy store. He and his friends called this "The Great Mouse Plot of 1924." He would later write about this candy in his story *The Everlasting Gobstopper*.

d  Perhaps the greatest inspiration from his childhood came from his time at Repton School for Boys. Situated nearby was the Cadbury's Chocolate Factory. Occasionally they would send samples of chocolate for the boys at the school to test. Roald Dahl dreamed of the day he would design a new chocolate bar that would impress Mr. Cadbury. Later on this was the inspiration for him to write *Charlie and the Chocolate Factory*.

e  In later life, he went on to write some of the most famous children's stories of all time. Even now, over 25 years after his death, his stories are as magical and popular as ever.

**B** Read the article again. True (T) or false (F)?

1. The writer couldn't understand how Roald Dahl could be so imaginative before he visited the museum.
2. Roald Dahl's first children's story was about a cake.
3. Roald Dahl's inspiration for his children's stories only came from his own childhood.
4. He wrote a story about a candy shop when he was only eight years old.
5. Cadbury's Chocolate Factory would involve the boys at his school in chocolate production.
6. The writer thinks Roald Dahl's stories still have universal appeal today.

**C** Circle the correct option.

1. Timothy leaned forward and *sniffed / fidgeted* the mug – the warm, sweet smell of chocolate.
2. Feeling nervous and not knowing what to do with her hands, Lucinda *clasped / cocked* them behind her back.
3. I tried to remain calm, but my *bustling / twitching* eye gave me away.
4. As she looked towards me, her eyelids *fidgeted / fluttered*, and she smiled.
5. Sit still George, and stop *fidgeting / fluttering*!

# What do you think of graffiti art?  6.4

**A** ▶ 25 Complete the conversation with the missing auxiliaries. Listen to check.

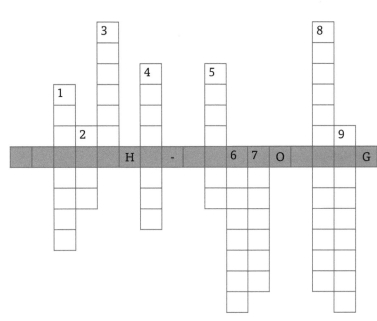

LISA: Have you seen that exhibit at the Museum of Modern Art yet?
RAFAEL: No, and I really ¹_____ not like modern art. It's just so pointless and easy.
LISA: I know what you mean. It ²_____ seem like that sometimes, doesn't it? But there's often more to it than meets the eye. You just have to be open to it.
RAFAEL: I ³_____ open to it! So, tell me what you mean.
LISA: OK, well take Jackson Pollock's work, for example. At first, his paintings just look like random blotches of paint.
RAFAEL: They ⁴_____ look like that, yes.
LISA: But, actually, his work contains what are called "fractals," which are infinitely complex mathematical patterns. He created them by very carefully dripping paint on the canvas. And they've been analyzed by computer software to show this. I bet you weren't aware of that.
RAFAEL: Wow, I ⁵_____ know that! Maybe I'll go and check out this exhibit after all.

**B** Replace the underlined words in each statement with auxiliaries as rejoinders.
1 I really <u>liked</u> the exhibit, even though I didn't say so. _____
2 Karla<u>'s been</u> working really hard lately. You just haven't seen her. _____
3 Wow, James <u>likes</u> graffiti art, doesn't he? _____
4 My mom<u>'s open</u> to me studying art at college, though she'd prefer it if I studied business. _____
5 You really <u>hated</u> the show, didn't you? _____

**C** Use the clues to complete the word puzzle with the adjectives from **7D** in the Students' Book. Guess the word in the shaded boxes.

1 interesting and full of variety
2 boring
3 very good, especially in an unexpected way
4 involving lots of new ideas
5 very strange
6 different from anything before
7 exciting, full of life
8 without new ideas, repetitive
9 makes you want to do something

## 6.5 Are musicals popular where you live?

**A** Read the book review. Which of these adjectives would the writer NOT use to describe the story?

☐ bizarre   ☐ funny   ☐ thought-provoking

### THE HUMANS  Matt Haig

Science fiction is a crowded genre, with many different books available. ¹ ☐ And it does this with a somewhat absurd, but at the same time believable, storyline.

The plot centers around Professor Andrew Martin of Cambridge University. ² ☐ However, he's not alone, and by no means the first to have done so. His actions are observed by a remote alien race, observing him from afar, one of whom is sent to earth to assassinate him. The alien race, believing that humans are incapable of handling such knowledge responsibly, feels that unless this matter is dealt with swiftly, the results will be disastrous.

The alien being tasked with the mission arrives on Earth bewildered and disgusted by humans, but as he comes to learn more about them, gradually learns to love them. ³ ☐

I won't say any more about what happens in order not to spoil the experience for you. ⁴ ☐ It's written with a broad audience in mind and is full of suspense, a real page-turner. At the end of the book, the "alien" gives us a list of 87 pieces of advice, gleaned from his experience during his time on our planet. Though meant to be humorous, it is at the same time insightful and moving, with such gems as, "Don't think you know, know you think."

I wholeheartedly recommend *The Humans* to anyone who not only enjoys an amusing read, but also enjoys something that can inspire all of us to think deeply about what it is to be human.

**B** Complete the review with extracts a–d.

a Alone in his office one night, he discovers the secret of prime numbers, a mathematical anomaly which allows him to unlock the secrets of the universe.

b Haig is a master at describing the human race in terms of both positive and negative traits, and you are left reassessing everything you thought you knew about what it is to be human.

c What I will say is that this book is a hilarious read, and contains colorful and insightful descriptions of human behavior from start to finish.

d What's really unique about this book, though, is the perspective it has on our everyday lives, viewed from an outsider.

**C** Match techniques 1–4 to extracts a–d in B.

1 ☐ praising the author
2 ☐ using descriptive adjectives
3 ☐ contrasting the book with others like it
4 ☐ offering plot details

**D** Look back at lessons 6.1–6.5 in the Student's Book. Find the connection between the song lines and the content of each lesson.

**E** ▶ 26 Listen to the five question titles from the unit, and record your answers to them. If possible, compare recordings with a classmate.

# Selected audio scripts

## 1 page 3 exercises A and B

J = Janet, C = Chris

J: So Chris, is it true that your nephew Simon is starting college next month?
C: Yes! Amazing, isn't it? I still think of him as being a child, but he was eighteen this year.
J: Tell me about it. I remember his first day at school. I can still see it as if it were yesterday.
C: That reminds me. Did I ever tell you about my first day at college?
J: No?
C: Oh, it was a complete nightmare!
J: Why? What happened?
C: Well, I was really, really tired. As far as I can remember, there'd been a party the night before for all the new students, and I must have gotten to bed in the early hours. Anyway, my alarm didn't go off so I woke up late and was rushing to get to the first class. I had just enough time to get a strong cup of coffee and that woke me up enough to get to class on time ... just barely.
J: That was lucky.
C: Yeah. So anyway, about halfway through the class the effects of the coffee wore off, and I have a vague recollection of the lecturer, a young woman, speaking in a really soft voice, and ... well, I must have dozed off at the back of the class.
J: Oh no! Did the lecturer see you?
C: Ha! Oh no, it was much worse than that. Suddenly, the alarm on my phone went off. I must have set it for the wrong time the night before or something, and I jumped up in my seat, and shouted ...
J: What did you say?
C: This is so embarrassing. I shouted out, "Don't make me get up yet, Mom!" – looking right at the lecturer!
J: Oh no! Why on earth did you say that?
C: I really don't know. I must have been half asleep still, or something. As you can imagine, everyone in the class started laughing.
J: What did the lecturer say?
C: Oh, nothing really, she just looked really embarrassed. I think she was more embarrassed than me, to be honest.
J: I can imagine.
C: Anyway, as soon as the class ended, I rushed off before anyone could talk to me.
J: Oh, you poor thing.
C: I know! But come to think of it, there was a happy ending. I became good friends with that lecturer, and in the end we had a laugh about it. She even jokingly called me her "little boy" in the class!
J: Well, I hope your nephew has a better first day than you.
C: Me too!

## 5 page 8 exercise A

C = Charlotte, G = Gavin

C: What's up, Gavin? You seem a bit down.
G: Oh, the usual. My job.
C: What? I thought you were really enjoying it there.
G: I used to, but I've been having a really tough time there lately. I must have done something to upset my boss, because he's making things really difficult for me.
C: How so?
G: Well, he's really critical of everything I do. And he keeps giving me really tight deadlines, which he knows I won't be able to meet. It feels like he just wants to make things hard for me every day.
C: That's really too bad. So, what are you going to do?
G: I have no idea. No, actually, that's not true. I've been toying with the idea of leaving, to be honest. It's just that the job pays well, and, uh, they're helping me work towards a Master's degree.
C: OK, but is that really what you want to do?
G: I thought so, but these days I'm not so sure.
C: All right, well, if you could do anything, what would you do?
G: Well, there is one thing ...

## 6 page 8 exercises B and C

G: Well, there is one thing...
C: What's that?
G: I know it sounds a little far-fetched, but I'm in a band with some old school friends.
C: Oh yes, *Robot Republic*! I saw you play the other week! You were great!
G: They want me to go on tour with them over the summer. But I don't know, I mean, I'd have to leave my job and my studies. And there's a lot at stake.
C: Yes, I think you're right. Being in the band is fun and everything, but what would you do after the tour? You can't just sit around and wait for something else to fall into your lap.
G: You're right, of course. That would be really reckless. It's just that with all my problems at work, succeeding there and finishing my degree – they just seem like really unattainable goals right now.
C: Have you tried talking to your boss about how you feel?
G: Do you think that's a good idea? Maybe it will just make things worse.
C: I can't see how. Maybe he's just under a lot of pressure himself. Perhaps you could take some vacation to go on the tour. Then when you come back, you'll be feeling refreshed. You'll go the extra mile and work better. You can still work toward your degree, and, hopefully you'll be feeling better about everything.
G: You really think so?
C: It can't hurt to try. I know if you put your mind to it, you can make things work.
G: I guess, you're right. Thanks so much, Charlotte. I'm feeling much better. I'm determined to try to make this work.
C: That's the spirit!

## 10 page 13 exercises A, B and C

V = Valeria, L = Leon, J = Julia

V: All in all, it's been a bit of a bumpy ride to be honest. I mean, for a long time when I first started, I couldn't even get a half-decent sound out of it, and felt really out of my depth. My teacher was really encouraging though, and I put a lot of effort into it, practicing every day. I gradually started to improve, until I was about intermediate level. Then when I went to college it fell by the wayside, and I just sort of stopped playing. I recently picked it up again, and although I was a bit rusty at first, soon it all came back to me. It's surprising how much you remember after you've learned it once. It's a bit like riding a bike, I guess. In the last year I've been playing more and more, and next week I have my first concert!
L: Well, about a year ago I went to the doctor for a check-up, and he told me I needed to start doing more exercise. I'd never been much of a "sports" person, and although it's a necessary evil, I'd always hated the thought of doing any exercise. So we talked about it, and he suggested that I try going for a walk every day. That seemed doable to me, so I gave it a try. It was actually surprisingly easy and in the end it opened up a whole new world. Before I knew it I was going longer distances each day and enjoying it more and more. I was hooked! Then I started jogging, and to my surprise, I just sort of picked it up naturally. Since then I've joined a club, and I've improved by leaps and bounds. Actually, I just signed up for my first half marathon in September!
J: I've always been into computers and technology, but never really known how they work. People see me as a sort of "techy" person, but I think that's debatable. I always just sort of get by when I need to and hope for the best. Well, a few months ago I decided to sign up for a free online course in coding because I thought it looked interesting, and I absolutely loved it. Most people think it's boring, but to me it's fun, fun, fun! I'm now writing my own stuff and have just produced my first app: it helps language learners record new vocabulary they see in signs in the street.

## 14 page 18 exercises A and B

S = Sue, J = Jaylan

J: Hey Sue, have you read this article about dreams?
S: No, what does it say?
J: Well apparently, there are several things that influence your dreams, and some are quite unexpected.
S: Oh really? I always take these things with a grain of salt. It's usually some nonsense about what star sign you are or something.
J: I know what you mean, but not this one. It's based on several scientific studies so the results are generally trustworthy.
S: So, what does it say?

63

# Selected audio scripts

J: Well, for example, bad smells can make you have bad dreams, and vice-versa.
S: Hmm, that sounds plausible.
J: Yes, according to a German study, 15 volunteers were asked to sleep in a laboratory in two groups. When they entered R.E.M. sleep–
S: R.E.M. sleep?
J: "Rapid Eye Movement." It's the stage of the sleep when you dream.
S: Oh, OK.
J: So, anyway, when they entered that, one group had foul smells pumped into the room and the other had nice smells pumped into theirs. After a few minutes they woke them up and asked them to immediately describe their dreams. And what they found was that there was a direct correlation – the nicer the smell, the nicer the dream!
S: That sounds logical. I mean, there's no doubt in my mind that strong smells have a big effect on how I feel. Especially when you don't take a shower after the gym!
J: Ha, without a shadow of a doubt. Sorry!
S: So, what else does it say?
J: Well, another study showed that regular video game players are able to take control of their dreams while asleep. It's called Lucid dreaming, and it's where dreams become lifelike. You're able to "fight off" bad dreams and take control. Just like in a video game!
S: Oh I see. How very convenient for you. I bet you're going to say next that it means you need to spend more time playing video games in the evening, right?
J: Well, I wouldn't go so far as to say that, but you know, if you think it's a good idea …
S: So, does it say anything about personality types? Or if dreams are stress-related?
J: Well, there is one thing. The jury is still out on this, but some scientists have made the claim that the more creative you are, the more likely you are to remember your dreams.
S: Now you see this is what I mean about articles about dreams. I mean, how do they define "creative"?
J: Yeah, I'm with you on this. It does seem very arbitrary. In the study they classified people according to things like how often they daydream or how imaginative they are. Not very results-oriented or objective if you ask me. Although maybe there is some truth in it. If you spend a lot of time when you're awake daydreaming and think about imaginary worlds, perhaps your brain finds it easier to move between the conscious and subconscious?
S: Listen to yourself!
J: What? I mean it! Look, why don't you take a look at the article yourself? It's very reader-friendly.
S: You know, I think I will. Believe it or not, it actually sounds quite interesting.

## ▶ 18 page 23 exercises A and B

M = Marta, L = Liam

M: What's that you're looking at, Liam?
L: It's an online article. It's really quite funny actually.
M: Yeah? What's it about?
L: It's about epic publicity stunts which ended up going badly. Do you want to hear about some?
M: Ooh, yes, please go on.
L: So way back in 1981, American Airlines launched the "AApass". The idea was that you pay a one-time price of $250,000, and then you have unlimited first-class tickets for the rest of your life.
M: A quarter of a million dollars? That's a lot!
L: Yes, but first-class tickets are expensive too. Think how many times you could fly in a lifetime if you wanted to. And that's exactly what customers did. Things got out of hand when customers with the ticket started flying very frequently. One guy flew to London sixteen times – in a month!
M: Wow!
L: Yes, and another frequent flier built up over 50 million air miles. Quite ironic really, since American Airlines invented frequent flyer programs.
M: So what happened?
L: Well, in the end, they realized it was a major oversight not to have anticipated customer reactions and decided to call the whole thing off. They stopped offering it in 1994.
M: Back to square one for them then! What else is there?
L: Let me see… OK, this is another good one. Have you heard of LifeLock?
M: Sure, they're the identity theft protection company, right?
L: Exactly. Well back in 2007, the CEO was so confident of their security that he published his own social security number on the website.
M: You're kidding!
L: Nope! It was a high-stakes plan, and one that fell flat on its face, too. Can you guess what happened?
M: Someone stole his identity?
L: Yes, but not just once. Thirteen times! The thieves used it to get loans and buy presents. He only found out when they called him up to ask about payment of the debt.
M: Oh dear. So his plans to demonstrate how secure the company was definitely fell through.
L: Exactly. This one is quite interesting, too. It's not so much of a publicity stunt, but it's definitely a publicity disaster.
M: Tell me.
L: So in London, there's a skyscraper in the center of the city which has a unique curved design. People call it the "walkie-talkie" because that's what it looks like. It's a huge building and cost over $250 million to build.
M: OK.
L: When they were on the verge of completing it, they noticed a glitch.
M: What was that?
L: For up to two hours every day in the summer, if the sun shines directly onto part of the building, the curved glass acts like a mirror, and sends really hot air down to the street.
M: Oh no, really?
L: Yes, and I mean really hot. Temperatures of up to 91 degrees centigrade were recorded, and it actually melted parts of cars!
M: Wow!
L: One reporter at the time was also able to fry an egg in a pan on the ground, it was that hot. But the best thing was that the building got a new nickname.
M: What's that?
L: The "fryscraper"!

## ▶ 22 page 28 exercises A and B

K = Kristin, N = Narrator

K: Hi everyone, and welcome to my webinar on how to become a successful online content writer. As we all know, people read websites differently from traditional books and journals. In a world where there's a multitude of free online articles, being a successful content writer means creating stunning content which people will pick out to read. Choosing a great topic will only get you so far – unless the actual content is sufficiently enjoyable to read, readers won't make it past the first paragraph. Today, I'm going to show you how to write content that brings out the best of your work.
N: Styles.
K: Successful content writers are able to work out how to write in the appropriate style for the medium. "Listicles" – those articles that have titles like "10 misconceptions people have about English", for example, are often friendly and informal. Opinion pieces, on the other hand, are often persuasive and well-researched, pointing out facts that support your argument. And that brings me to my next piece of advice …
N: Research.
K: You should always keep your research mode turned on. When you're browsing the Internet for ideas or facts, keep a bank of links to use as sources. Make sure your sources are reliable by cross-checking any facts with at least two other sources, or you might even want to delete the fact. You can just cross it out and start again.
N: Your voice.
K: While it's important to understand the key features of different styles, it's also important to craft your own unique voice. Whether it's through the things you write about or the way you say them, it's important to be original. People should be able to recognize your writing before they see your name on the page. Once you've realized that, you'll never wear out your welcome.
N: Social media.
K: Finally, once you've written your unique content, you need to get it out there. Successful content writers know how to promote themselves through social media. You should have your own, professional account on each platform, which can be tagged onto anything you write. It will also help you build a professional network to showcase your work.

# Answer key

## Unit 1

### 1.1
A a 2  b 5  c 1  d 4  e 3
B 1 T  2 F  3 F  4 T  5 F
C 1 wore off  2 took off  3 pull off
   4 doze off  5 ring  5 rushed off
D Students' own answers

### 1.2
A 1 is  2 taste  3 has  4 seems  5 say
B 1 vary  2 fail  3 seems  4 has  5 takes
   6 helps  7 is  8 have  9 discovers
   10 make
C Possible answers: 1 isn't  2 thinks
   3 doesn't like  4 is  5 have been
D Students' own answers

### 1.3
A It has bad advice (for those who want to work well).
B 1 It has to be perfect.  2 Don't be rude.
   3 Always work in the same place.
   4 Keep up with the world.
   5 Question everything.
C 1 mind **wander** for a while
   2 keep tuning **out**  3 it hit **me**
   4 zero **in** on  5 pop **into** her head
   6 stay on **top** of things

### 1.4
A 1 have been  2 've seen  3 had made
   4 had been trying  5 have described
   6 had ever done  7 haven't watched
   8 created
B 1 has  2 had  3 has had
   4 hasn't helped  5 have come  6 had
   7 has
C 1 c  2 d  3 a  4 e  5 b

### 1.5
A 1 I'd just finished  2 had been snowing
   3 had just stopped  4 had driven  5 saw
   6 was  7 had been looking  8 went
   9 got  10 We've had
B 1 nothing but sheer  2 I did nothing but
   3 all but certain  4 couldn't help but
C 1 face, for  2 asking, know  3 what, give
D 1 phrasal verb with *off: shake it off*
   2 the grammar: subject-verb agreement (collective nouns)
   3 creativity
   4 the grammar: using perfect tenses
   5 a dream that came true
E Students' own answers

## Unit 2

### 2.1
A 1 no  2 He's critical.  3 leaving his job
   4 no
B To go on tour with his band. Yes, she encourages him to do it.
C 1 far-fetched  2 fall, lap  3 unattainable goals  4 extra mile  5 work toward
   6 put, mind

D 1 Go the extra mile
   2 Never try to meet people's expectations
   3 If you put your mind to it
   4 don't wait for them to fall into your lap
E 1 c  2 e  3 b  4 a

### 2.2
A 1 have  2 to  3 don't  4 isn't  5 hasn't
B 1 too, are, didn't, They're  2 might, have
   3 take  4 to, haven't, didn't
C 1 doesn't  2 have  3 does  4 either
   5 might
D Students' own answers

### 2.3
A 1 B  2 D  3 A  4 C
B 1 Ella  2 the extra statement  3 Jerome
   4 Alison  5 Brynn
C 1 crave, peace and quiet  2 convey, sense of  3 cater, tastes  4 upscale, restaurants

### 2.4
A 1 so  2 such  3 so, such  4 so  5 so
   6 so
B 1 b  2 c  3 c  4 a  5 b  6 a
C 1 ~~so much~~ so many  2 ~~such big~~ such a big
   3 ~~so~~ so much  4 ~~such~~ so much
D 1 drowsy  2 boost  3 dragging  4 hectic
   5 sleep
E Students' own answers

### 2.5
A He likes them both.
B 1 each has its pros and cons  2 In addition
   3 However  4 on the other hand
   5 Although  6 the two areas are both
C 1 has its pros and cons
   2 In addition, it has a swimming pool.
   3 Our dining room, on the other hand / On the other hand, our dining room
   4 are both cheap places to live.
D 1 being guided to a goal  2 the importance of home  3 being alone  4 the grammar: using *so many* and *so much*  5 comparing apartments
E Students' own answers

## Unit 3

### 3.1
A Valeria: 3  Leon: 6  Julia: 5
B 1 Julia  2 Valeria  3 Leon  4 Julia
   5 Valeria  6 Leon
C 1 depth  2 effort  3 rusty  4 picked
   5 leaps  6 debatable  7 get
D Students' own answers

### 3.2
A Students' own answers
B 1 What this means is to
   2 we think relates back to
   3 Why this became so popular
   4 What's interesting is that
   5 Where it came from was

   6 What it would do was
   7 What we know about this expression is
   8 we don't really know
C 1 d,S  2 e,O  3 a,O  4 b,S  5 c,S
D 1 extent  2 least  3 will  4 respects
E Students' own answers

### 3.3
A 1 The Motivator  2 The Entertainer
   3 The Storyteller  4 The Animator
   5 The Lecturer
B 1 F  2 NI  3 NI  4 T  5 T
C 1 spread the word  2 keep your word  3 by word of mouth  4 take back your words  5 have the final word  6 tripping over words  7 get a word in edgewise

### 3.4
A 1 Growing up  2 Starting  3 Encouraged
   4 Arriving  5 meeting  6 Feeling
B 1 Before becoming famous
   2 Growing up in Pennsylvania
   3 Working as a support act
   4 Hoping to become a soccer player
   5 Signing her first modeling contract
C 1 ~~learn~~ learned  2 ~~Where~~ When  3 ~~had~~ having  4 ~~hearing~~ heard  5 ~~taking~~ taken
D Students' own answers

### 3.5
A c
B 1 b  2 a  3 d
C 1 beginning  2 while  3 time  4 Then
   5 First  6 matter
D 1 foreign languages
   2 slang expressions
   3 words and self-expression
   4 the grammar: how parents help/influence their children
   5 accomplishing something if you try
E Students' own answers

## Unit 4

### 4.1
A 2, 5 and 6
B 1 15  2 dream  3 control  4 fight
   5 remember  6 daydream
C 1 ~~gram~~ grain  2 ~~worry~~ doubt  3 ~~With~~ Without  4 ~~long~~ far  5 ~~judge~~ jury
D 1 b  2 e  3 a  4 f  5 c  6 d

### 4.2
A 1 Little did I know
   2 Never again will I be late
   3 rarely does my staff play
   4 Not since my previous job had I worked
   5 did I understand
B 1 Nowhere could I find my keyboard!
   2 Only after I got home did I realize I had the wrong bag.
   3 Rarely do we play April Fool's Day pranks in my country.

# Answer key

4 Little did he know, we'd switched his laptop for a pizza box!
5 Not since I was a teenager had I felt so embarrassed.
C 1 wreaking  2 breathe  3 clogged  4 flee
D Students' own answers

## 4.3
A 1
B 1 b  2 c  3 a  4 a  5 b
C 1 break-in  2 throwaway  3 wipeout  4 crackdown  5 cover-up  6 tip-off  7 takeover
D Students' own answers

## 4.4
A 1 e  2 b  3 d  4 c  5 a
B 1 in which  2 whom  3 about which  4 towards which  5 which  6 most of whom
C 1 S,S  2 S,Z  3 Z,S  4 S,Z

## 4.5
A 1 c  2 e  3 a  4 d  5 f  6 b
B 1 debate  2 strongly  3 irrespective  4 claims  5 argue
C 1 the truth always comes out  2 on the table  3 up to us  4 conceal information  5 banned from
D 1 dreams (vs. reality)  2 the grammar: emphatic inversion  3 illogical vs. logical thinking  4 our eyes and our emotions  5 the value of freedom (vs. incarceration)
E Students' own answers

## Unit 5
### 5.1
A 1 T  2 F  3 T  4 F
B 1 the year the AApass was launched
2 the cost of the AApass, in dollars
3 the number of air miles one passenger accumulated
4 the year they stopped selling the AApass
5 the year the CEO of LifeLock published his social security number on the company website
6 the number of times his identity was stolen
7 the cost of the "walkie talkie" building in dollars
8 the temperature recorded on the street
C 1 oversight, call  2 stakes  3 through  4 verge, glitch
D 1 pull  2 face  3 one  4 to  5 hand
E Students' own answers

### 5.2
A 1 Given  2 as  3 aim  4 effort  5 Thanks  6 view
B 1 c  2 b  3 e  4 a  5 d
C 1 fresh  2 get  3 through  4 anew  5 page  6 to
D Students' own answers

### 5.3
A 2
B 1 Vanda  2 Steve  3 extra comment  4 Steve  5 Carla
C 1 held on to  2 took stock  3 went to great lengths  4 dwell on  5 keep (things) in perspective  6 put (failures) behind you
D Students' own answers

### 5.4
A Possible answers: 1 me / my  2 the government's / insurance companies'  3 people / women  4 this person's / his  5 her / my date's
B 1 is  2 who  3 they them  4 made making / to make  5 he's him
C 1 with  2 out  3 on, up  4 off  5 to, up

### 5.5
A 1
B 1 Broadly speaking  2 Essentially  3 Clearly  4 Admittedly  5 Incidentally  6 Obviously  7 Frankly
C 1 entail  2 airtight, spells out  3 put together, turned it down, redo it
D 1 failure / letting someone down
2 New Year's Day and resolutions / the grammar: not using formal conjunctions and prepositions  3 effort and not being successful  4 relationships  5 bad drivers
E Students' own answers

## Unit 6
### 6.1
A 1 b  2 d  3 a  4 c
B 1 a  2 c  3 c  4 b  5 a
C 1 pick out  2 brings out  3 work out  4 pointing out  5 cross (it) out  6 wear out
D Students' own answers

### 6.2
A 1 Unless  2 even if  3 in case  4 as long as  5 whether or not
B 1 in case  2 as long as  3 unless  4 whether or not  5 even if
C 1 the theater  2 curiosity  3 sync  4 10  5 patience  6 sheer habit
D Students' own answers

### 6.3
A 1 c  2 a  3 e  4 d  5 extra topic  6 b
B 1 T  2 F  3 F  4 F  5 T  6 T
C 1 sniffed  2 clasped  3 twitching  4 fluttered  5 fidgeting

### 6.4
A 1 do  2 does  3 am  4 do  5 didn't
B 1 did like  2 has been  3 does like  4 is open  5 did hate
C 1 colorful  2 dull  3 amazing  4 creative  5 bizarre  6 original  7 vibrant  8 unimaginative  9 inspiring
Word: thought-provoking

### 6.5
A bizarre
B 1 d  2 a  3 b  4 c
C 1 b  2 c  3 d  4 a
D 1 paper books (and not electronic ones)
2 using *out of*  3 expressions with *heaven* (Roald Dahl title)  4 the grammar: using auxiliaries as rejoinders  5 dreams (and the immigrant experience)
E Students' own answers

# Phrasal verb list

Phrasal verbs are verbs with two or three words: main verb + particle (either a preposition or an adverb). The definitions given below are some of those introduced in iDentities. For a full list, visit www.richmondidentites.com

## Transitive phrasal verbs have a direct object; some are separable, others inseparable

| Phrasal verb | Meaning |
|---|---|
| **A** | |
| **ask** someone **over** | invite someone |
| **B** | |
| **block** something **out** | prevent from passing through (light, noise) |
| **blow** something **out** | extinguish (a candle) |
| **bring** something **about** | cause to happen |
| **bring** something **out** | introduce a new product |
| **bring** someone **up** | raise (a child) |
| **bring** something **up** | bring to someone's attention |
| **C** | |
| **call** someone **in** | ask for someone's presence |
| **call** something **off** | cancel |
| **carry** something **out** | conduct an experiment / plan |
| **cash in on** something | profit |
| **catch up on** something | get recent information |
| **charge** something **up** | charge with electricity |
| **check** someone / something **out** | examine closely |
| **check up on** someone | make sure a person is OK |
| **cheer** someone **up** | make happier |
| **clear** something **up** | clarify |
| **come away with** something | learn something useful |
| **come down to** something | be the most important point |
| **come down with** something | get an illness |
| **come up with** something | invent |
| **count on** someone / something | depend on |
| **crack down on** something | take severe measures |
| **cut** something **down** | bring down (a tree); reduce |
| **cut** someone **off** | interrupt someone |
| **cut** something **off** | remove; stop the supply of |
| **cut** something **out** | remove; stop doing an action |
| **D** | |
| **do** something **over** | do again |
| **draw** something **together** | unite |
| **dream** something **up** | invent |
| **drop** someone / something **off** | take someplace |
| **drop out of** something | quit |
| **dwell on** something | linger over, think hard about something |
| **E** | |
| **end up with** something | have an unexpected result |
| **F** | |
| **face up to** something | accept something unpleasant |
| **fall back on** something | use an old idea |
| **fall for** someone | feel romantic love |
| **fall for** something | be tricked into believing |
| **figure** someone / something **out** | understand with thought |
| **fill** someone **in** | explain |
| **find** something **out** | learn information |
| **follow** something **through** | complete |
| **G** | |
| **get** something **across** | help someone understand |
| **get around to** something | finally do something |
| **get away with** something | avoid the consequences |
| **get off** something | leave (a bus, train, plane) |
| **get on** something | board (a bus, train, plane) |
| **get out of** something | leave (a car); avoid doing something |
| **get to** someone | upset someone |

| Phrasal verb | Meaning |
|---|---|
| **get to** something | reach |
| **get together with** someone | meet |
| **give** something **back** | return |
| **give** something **up** | quit |
| **give up on** someone / something | stop hoping for change / trying to make something happen |
| **go along with** something | agree |
| **grow out of** something | stop doing (over time, as one becomes an adult) |
| **H** | |
| **hand** something **in** | submit |
| **hand** something **out** | distribute |
| **help** someone **out** | assist |
| **K** | |
| **keep** someone or something **away** | cause to stay at a distance |
| **keep** something **on** | not remove (clothing / jewelry) |
| **keep** someone or something **out** | prevent from entering |
| **keep up with** someone | stay in touch |
| **L** | |
| **lay** someone **off** | fire for economic reasons |
| **lay** something **out** | arrange |
| **leave** something **on** | not turn off (a light or appliance); not remove (clothing or jewelry) |
| **leave** something **out** | not include, omit |
| **let** someone **down** | disappoint |
| **let** someone **off** | allow to leave (a bus, train); not punish |
| **light** something **up** | illuminate |
| **look after** someone / something | take care of |
| **look down on** someone | think one is better, disparage |
| **look into** something | research |
| **look out for** someone | watch, protect |
| **look** someone / something **up** | try to find |
| **look up to** someone | admire, respect |
| **M** | |
| **make** something **up** | invent |
| **make up for** something | do something to apologize |
| **miss out on** something | lose the chance |
| **P** | |
| **pass** something **out** | distribute |
| **pass** someone / something **up** | reject, not use |
| **pay** someone **back** | repay, return money |
| **pay** someone **off** | bribe |
| **pay** something **off** | pay a debt |
| **pick** someone **up** | give someone a ride |
| **pick** something **up** | get / buy; learn something; answer the phone; get a disease |
| **point** someone / something **out** | indicate, show |
| **pull** something **off** | make something happen |
| **put** something **away** | return to its appropriate place |
| **put** something **back** | return to its original place |
| **put** someone **down** | treat with disrespect |
| **put** something **off** | delay |
| **put** something **together** | assemble, build |
| **put** something **up** | build, erect |
| **put up with** someone / something | accept without complaining |

119

# Phrasal verb list

| Phrasal verb | Meaning |
|---|---|
| **R** | |
| **run into** someone | meet |
| **run out of** something | not have enough |
| **run** something **by** someone | tell someone something so they can give you their opinion |
| **S** | |
| **see** something **through** | complete |
| **send** something **back** | return |
| **send** something **out** | mail |
| **set** something **up** | establish; prepare for use |
| **settle on** something | choose after consideration |
| **show** someone / something **off** | display the best qualities |
| **shut** something **off** | stop (a machine, light, supply) |
| **sign** someone **up** | register |
| **stand up for** someone / something | support |
| **stick with / to** someone / something | not quit, persevere |
| **straighten** something **up** | make neat |
| **switch** something **on** | start, turn on (a machine, light) |
| **T** | |
| **take over from** someone | take control from someone else |
| **take** something **away** | remove |
| **take** something **back** | return; accept an item; retract a statement |
| **take** something **in** | notice, remember; make a clothing item smaller |
| **take** someone **on** | hire |
| **take** something **on** | agree to a task |
| **take** someone **out** | invite and pay for someone |
| **take** something **up** | start a new activity (as a habit) |
| **talk** someone **into** | persuade |
| **talk** something **over** | discuss |
| **tear** something **down** | destroy, demolish |
| **tear** something **up** | tear into small pieces |
| **think back on** something | remember |
| **think** something **over** | consider |
| **think** something **up** | invent, think of a new idea |
| **tip** someone **off** | give someone a hint or warning |
| **touch** something **up** | improve with small changes |
| **try** something **on** | put on to see if it fits, is desirable (clothing, shoes) |
| **try** something **out** | use an item / do an activity to see if it's desirable |
| **turn** something **around** | turn so the front faces the back; cause to get better |
| **turn** someone / something **down** | reject |
| **turn** something **in** | submit |
| **turn** someone / something **into** | change from one type or form to another |
| **turn** someone **off** | cause to lose interest, feel negatively |
| **turn** something **out** | make, manufacture |
| **U** | |
| **use** something **up** | use completely, consume |
| **W** | |
| **wake** someone **up** | cause to stop sleeping |
| **walk out on** someone | leave a spouse / child / romantic relationship |
| **warm (up) to** something/someone | begin to like something or someone |
| **watch out for** someone | protect |
| **wear** someone/something **out** | damage from too much use |
| **wipe** something **out** | remove, destroy |
| **work** something **out** | calculate mathematically; solve a problem |
| **write** something **down** | create a written record (on paper) |
| **write** something **up** | write in a finished form |

## Intransitive phrasal verbs
have no direct object; they are all inseparable

| | |
|---|---|
| **A** | |
| **act up** | behave inappropriately |
| **B** | |
| **blow over** | pass, be forgotten |
| **break down** | stop functioning |
| **break up** | end a relationship |
| **C** | |
| **catch on** | become popular |
| **check in** | report arrival (at a hotel, airport) |
| **check out** | pay a bill and leave (a hotel) |
| **cheer up** | become happier |
| **come along** | go with, accompany |
| **come up** | arise (an issue) |
| **D** | |
| **doze off** | fall asleep unintentionally |
| **dress up** | wear more formal clothes; a costume |
| **drop in** | visit unexpectedly |
| **drop out** | quit |
| **E** | |
| **eat out** | eat in a restaurant |
| **F** | |
| **fall through** | fail to happen |
| **find out** | learn new information |
| **follow through** | finish, complete something |
| **G** | |
| **get ahead** | make progress, succeed |
| **get along** | have a good relationship |
| **get by** | survive |
| **get through** | finish; survive |
| **go along** | accompany; agree |
| **go away** | leave a place |
| **go on** | continue |
| **H** | |
| **hang up** | end a phone call |
| **hold on** | wait (often during a phone call) |
| **K** | |
| **keep away** | stay at a distance |
| **keep on** | continue |
| **keep up** | maintain speed / momentum |
| **L** | |
| **lie down** | recline (on a bed / floor / sofa) |
| **light up** | illuminate; look pleased, happy |
| **look out** | be careful |
| **M** | |
| **make up** | end an argument |
| **miss out** | lose the chance (for something good) |
| **P** | |
| **pass out** | become unconscious, faint |
| **pay off** | be worthwhile |
| **pick up** | improve |
| **pop up** | occur unexpectedly |
| **R** | |
| **run out** | leave suddenly; not have enough (a supply) |
| **S** | |
| **show up** | appear; arrive at a place |
| **sign up** | register |
| **slip up** | make a mistake |
| **stay up** | not go to bed |
| **T** | |
| **take off** | leave, depart (a plane); succeed, achieve success |
| **turn in** | go to sleep |
| **turn out** | have a certain result |
| **turn up** | appear |
| **W** | |
| **wear off** | disappear, diminish slowly |